MASTER OF INTUITION: SHERLOCK HOLMES

NOTES ON THE COMPLETE COLLECTION OF SHERLOCK HOLMES

TANG XUDONG

MASTER OF INTUITION: SHERLOCK HOLMES
NOTES ON THE COMPLETE COLLECTION OF SHERLOCK HOLMES

iUniverse books may be ordered through booksellers or by contacting:

iUniverse
1663 Liberty Drive
Bloomington, IN 47403
www.iuniverse.com
844-349-9409

Because of the dynamic nature of the Internet, any web addresses or links contained in this book may have changed since publication and may no longer be valid. The views expressed in this work are solely those of the author and do not necessarily reflect the views of the publisher, and the publisher hereby disclaims any responsibility for them.

Any people depicted in stock imagery provided by Getty Images are models, and such images are being used for illustrative purposes only.
Certain stock imagery © Getty Images.

ISBN: 978-1-6632-5338-5 (sc)
ISBN: 978-1-6632-5339-2 (e)

Library of Congress Control Number: 2023909684

Print information available on the last page.

iUniverse rev. date: 05/23/2023

CONTENT INTRODUCTION

In the vast amount of research results on Sherlock Holmes, almost all eyes have focused on his logical reasoning, while the research on his intuitive thinking is rare. Even if it is mentioned in a few articles, it is just a skim, and there is no further elaboration and research.The main reason is that up to now, the academic circles have been arguing about the characteristics of intuitive thinking, and there is no universally recognized definition like logical thinking. It is precisely because of this that many scholars and enthusiasts are attracted to carry out in-depth discussion with the scientific spirit of "bold hypothesis and careful verification".More than 30 years ago, the author began to pay attention to this subject without any superficial knowledge, and has published relevant works, such as *Intuition: A Preliminary Exploration of Investigative Thinking* (1989), *Intuition: An Analysis of Investigative Thinking* (2017), *Intuitive Perspective of Detective Investigative Thinking* (October 2020, Jiangxi Higher Education Press), *The Charm of Intuition* (December 2021, Dixie W Publishing Corporation U.S.A), *100 Refined Cases of Intuitive Investigation* (January 2022, Dixie W Publishing Corporation U.S.A), etc. These works have made some discussions on intuitive thinking.Ma AI, president of the National Legal Psychology Research Association and professor of China University of Political Science and Law, once sent a group of six of his doctoral and master's students to conduct an exclusive interview on the author's intuition investigation thinking in december2021, which inspired and benefited the author a lot. With their encouragement, this year, the author boldly fulfilled his long cherished wish in the form of reading notes to explore Holmes' intuitive investigative thinking in the complete collection of Sherlock Holmes.

In relevant works, Holmes has a large number of intuitive expressions. For example, Holmes said, "You have been in Afghanistan, I perceive."

"How on earth did you know that?" Watson asked in astonishment.

First of all, Holmes explained the reason why he "knew": I knew you were coming back from Afghanistan as soon as I saw you. A series of thoughts quickly flitted through my mind, so when I came to a conclusion, I was unaware of the intermediate link - this is an important form of intuitive thinking - conclusion type. Holmes often uses this way to show the "divine operation" brought by his extraordinary intuitive ability and level, which we call "Sherlock Holmes' intuitive show". This kind of "intuition show" can be found everywhere, especially in 33 places, which is also a beautiful scenery in *Sherlock Holmes*.

Second, Holmes used a large number of words such as "guess", "conjecture" and "reckon", and there are numerous ways of thinking to measure the unknown according to the known. As the former Soviet Union criminal investigation expert Belkin said in his *A New Probe into the World's Strange Cases*: experienced investigators sometimes make correct guesses based on trivial evidence, some non substantive plots in the case and the details of the suspect's behavior. This phenomenon is called investigative intuition. This is another form of intuitive thinking: speculation type.

Third, Holmes had a large number of questions in the face of the complicated case, using words such as "doubt", "queer", "strange", "odd", "curious", "abnormal" and so on, and on this basis, he had a careful thinking. These belong to the third form of intuitive thinking: doubt type.

Fourth, after pondering over the case of "mountains and rivers have no way out", Holmes suddenly appeared the realm of "another village with a bright future", which made him enlightened. Such sudden thoughts and ideas are like lightning and flint, which are fleeting and can be met but not sought. This is a special form of intuitive thinking: epiphany type.

These are the factual and theoretical basis for this book to study, interpret and prove that Holmes is a well deserved master of intuition.

In addition, while studying Holmes, the book also makes appropriate comments on the words and deeds related to intuitive thinking of his close comrade in arms and "best friend" Watson, as well as several police officers and main parties, trying to understand our protagonist more comprehensively and profoundly from multiple angles and levels.

ABOUT THE AUTHOR

Tang Xudong, male, from Jiangxi, has a bachelor's degree. He is currently the academic consultant of Jiangxi Marginal Law Research Association, vice chairman of Jiangxi Law society, and vice chairman of Legal Psychology Research Association of Jiangxi Psychological Society. He used to be part-time instructor of "Investigative Psychology" of Jiangxi Police College, off campus master tutor of Applied Psychology Teaching and Research Office of Humanities College of Jiangxi University of Traditional Chinese Medicine, and off campus master tutor of Humanities College of East China Jiaotong University.

Related works: *Psychology of Female Offenders' Transformation* (Coauthor, Henan People's Publishing House, 1989), *Intuition: A Preliminary Study of Investigative Thinking, A Brief Discussion on Legal Thinking, Analysis of Interrogation Psychology of Corruption and Bribery Crimes, Psychology and Prevention of Job-related Crimes* (Deputy Editor-in-Chief, Suzhou University Publishing House, 2010), *Intuition: Analysis of Investigative Thinking, Intuitive Perspective of Detective Investigative Thinking* (Jiangxi Higher Education Publishing House, October 2020), *The Charm of Intuition* (December 2021, Dixie W Publishing Corporation U.S.A), *100 Cases of Intuitive Investigation* (January 2022, Dixie W Publishing Corporation U.S.A), etc. Relevant popular science works: *After Thinking Enters a Dead End, Poor Students' Thinking Is Not Bad, Communication Psychology, How Big is Your Measurement, Thinking After Regrets, 30 Kinds of Job-related Crime Psychology*, etc.

CONTENTS

PREFACE

The proposition of "Master of Intuition:Sherlock Holmes" was put forward when I gave a lecture to graduate students. A classmate said, "I've only heard of Holmes as a master of deduction, but I've never heard of Holmes as a master of intuition!"

"Yes, Holmes is actually a master of intuition first, and then a master of reasoning." I said, "Have you read *Sherlock Holmes*?"

"Yes! But that was during college. What impressed me most was the first novel in the book, *A Study in Scarlet.*"

"Do you remember what Holmes said when he met Watson?" I asked.

"Yes! As soon as Holmes saw Watson, he said, 'You have been in Afghanistan, I perceive.' Holmes' feeling is really magical!"

"This is the result of Sherlock Holmes' intuitive thinking. At that time, Watson was very surprised to ask Sherlock Holmes how he knew. The next step is the work of the reasoning master. Sherlock Holmes answered Watson how he knew by using the method of backtracking reasoning. That is to say, the intuition master is in front, and the reasoning master is behind."

Then, I shared with him my experience in learning *Sherlock Holmes*.

First of all, Holmes explained the reason why he "knew": I knew you were coming back from Afghanistan as soon as I saw you. A series of thoughts quickly flitted through my mind, so when I came to a conclusion, I was unaware of the intermediate link - this is an important form of intuitive thinking - conclusion type. Holmes often uses this way to show the "divine operation" brought by his extraordinary intuitive ability and level, which we call "Sherlock Holmes' intuitive show". This kind of "intuition show" can be found everywhere, especially in 33 places, which is also a beautiful scenery in *Sherlock Holmes*.Second, Holmes used a large number of words such as "guess", "conjecture" and "reckon", and there are numerous ways of thinking to measure the unknown according to the known. As the former Soviet Union criminal investigation expert Belkin said in his *A New Probe into the World's Strange Cases*: experienced investigators sometimes make correct guesses based on trivial evidence, some non substantive plots in the case and the details of the suspect's behavior. This phenomenon is called investigative intuition. This is another form of intuitive thinking: speculation type.Third, Holmes had a large number of questions in the face of the complicated case, using words such as "doubt", "queer", "strange", "odd", "curious", "abnormal" and so on, and on this basis, he had a careful thinking. These belong to the third form of intuitive thinking: doubt type. Fourth, after pondering over the case of "mountains and rivers have no way out", Holmes suddenly appeared the realm of "another village with a bright future", which made him enlightened. Such sudden thoughts and ideas are like lightning and flint, which are fleeting and can be met but not sought. This is a special form of intuitive thinking: epiphany type.These are the factual and theoretical basis for this book to study, interpret and prove that Holmes is a well deserved master of intuition.

In addition, while studying Holmes, the book also makes appropriate comments on the words and deeds related to intuitive thinking of his close comrade in arms and "best friend" Watson, as well as several police officers and main parties, trying to understand our protagonist more comprehensively and profoundly from multiple angles and levels.

In the vast amount of research results on Sherlock Holmes, almost all eyes have focused on his logical reasoning, while the research on his intuitive thinking is rare. Even if it is mentioned in a few articles, it is just a skim, and there is no further elaboration and research.The main reason is that up to now, the academic circles have been arguing about the characteristics of intuitive thinking, and there is no universally recognized definition like logical thinking. It is precisely because of this that many scholars and enthusiasts are attracted to carry out in-depth discussion with the scientific spirit of "bold hypothesis and careful verification".I began to pay attention to this topic more than 30 years ago, and have published relevant articles, such as *Intuition: A Preliminary Exploration of Investigative Thinking* (1989), and *Intuition: An Analysis of Investigative Thinking* (2017). In 2018, when collecting materials and preparing to write *Intuitive Perspective of Detective Investigation Thinking*, I thought that the theme of "intuitive master Holmes" was very worthy of study. After the publication of the book (by Jiangxi Higher Education Press) in October 2020, there was a fear of difficulties while considering further research.*Sherlock Holmes* is a world classic detective masterpiece. Since its first work, *A study in Scarlet*, was published in 1887, it has had a great impact on readers all over the world for more than a hundred years. Moreover, this classic is of great length, with a total of 4 novels and 56 short stories. I dare not act rashly for fear of desecrating the "gods" in people's hearts. So I had to continue to cultivate my own acre of land, wrote the charm of intuition from the perspective of the public, and published it in November 2021 (by Dixie W Publishing Corporation U.S.A). Two months later, in January 2022, *100 Refined Cases of Intuitive Investigation* was published (also by Dixie W Publishing Corporation U.S.A).

It is worth mentioning and expressing gratitude that in December 2021, Mr. Ma AI, president of the National Legal Psychology Research Association and professor of China University of Political Science and Law, led a group of six doctoral and master's students to talk with me in Nanchang, and jointly discussed the application of intuitive investigative thinking in judicial practice. I was greatly inspired and benefited a lot. Inspired by the spirit of this discussion, after the Spring Festival this year, I summoned up my courage and bravely tried to practice my long cherished wish in the form of reading notes to learn and explore Holmes' intuition - investigative thinking in the book *Sherlock Holmes*.

Master of Intuition Sherlock Holmes, in the form of notes, uses the principles of intuitive thinking to perspective and analyze Sherlock Holmes' investigative thinking, reproducing and restoring the thinking process during Sherlock Holmes' investigative process, and overturning people's understanding of Sherlock Holmes' investigative thinking over the past century.Due to my limited level of knowledge, it is inevitable that there are omissions and even errors in the book. I sincerely hope that readers, especially experts and scholars, can understand and provide valuable suggestions!

Intuitive Perspective of Detective Investigation Thinking is the first work of non logical investigation,*100 Cases of Intuitive Investigation* is the integration of non logical investigation case sets, while *Intuitive Charm* is their popular reading.The forthcoming *Sherlock Holmes, Master of Intuition*, is obviously an applied reading of non logical investigation, and is a close friend of investigators, detective enthusiasts and fans of Holmes.

Although this book "has nothing to do with fame and enterprising", it also hopes to become a paving stone to enter the "circle of friends" of Holmes lovers, with a view to seeing more experts and scholars who study and love Mr. Holmes in that sacred hall. I am willing to worship them as teachers and further explore this great and mysterious classic character under their guidance.

It is worth mentioning that in the process of writing this note, I have always received the warm help and support from associate professor Shuai Qinghua, doctor of law, and associate professor Shen Xunbing, doctor of psychology. I would like to express my heartfelt thanks to the two gentlemen!

On October 22, 2022, Moma, Nanchang

A STUDY IN SCARLET (NOVEL)

1. Being a Reprint From the Reminiscences of John H. Watson, M.D., Late of the Army Medical Department

AFTER BEING WOUNDED ON THE BATTLEFIELD, DR. WATSON RETURNED TO LONDON FOR recuperation. For financial reasons, he planned to move out of the hotel and find someone to share an apartment. One day, when he ran into his former assistant, young Stamford, he chatted about it. It happened that one of his friends had taken a fancy to an ideal apartment, but the price was a bit expensive, and he was looking for a suitable person to share it with. Therefore, young Stamford had to try to match it and help him complete this matter. Picking a date is worse than hitting a date. After they had lunch together, they couldn't wait to meet his friend. Along the way, young Stamford had to constantly vaccinate Watson and introduce his friend's "quirks" so that Watson would be fully prepared. Who is this friend of little Stanford? It turned out to be the famous and well-known "self-employed" detective Sherlock Holmes all over Europe.

A. Sherlock Holmes' Intuition Show (No.1)

"Dr. Watson, Mr. Sherlock Holmes," said young Stamford introducing us.

"How are you?" Mr. Sherlock Holmes said cordially, gripping my hand with a strength. "You have been in Afghanistan, I perceive."

"How on earth did you know that?" Watson asked in astonishment.

Then, Holmes explained why he "knew": I knew right away that you had come back from Afghanistan. As a long-established habit, a series of thoughts swept through my mind so quickly that I came to a conclusion without noticing the middle link———one

1

of the important manifestations of intuitive thinking. However, the conclusion is drawn step by step.

Holmes then explains how he "knew" his reasoning:

1. With the demeanor of a medical staff and a bit of a soldier's temperament, he is obviously a military doctor;
2. He has just returned from the tropics, for his complexion is dark, but his fair wrists shows that it is not his true color;
3. His face is haggard, evidently he has been through ordeal, and is afflicted by illness;
4. The movement of his left arm is a little stiff and unnatural, indicating that his left arm was injured.

Conclusion: a British military doctor suffered hardships and injured his arm. Which tropical region might this be in? Obviously in Afghanistan. The historical background of Britain and the second Afghanistan war is the knowledge base of this intuition.

From the above, we can clearly see that the first sentence of Holmes is the result of intuitive thinking, and the following paragraphs show logical thinking ——retrospective reasoning. People often only see the rigorous logical reasoning behind Holmes, not the intuitive thinking in front of him. As for the intuitive thinking used by Holmes and other personnel in the process of life and investigation, they turned a blind eye and a deaf ear. Let's read this classic handed down together and try to find out the wonderful fragments of Holmes' intuitive thinking. While appreciating Holmes' thoughtful and wonderful reasoning, we also enjoy the amazing "divine operation" brought by Holmes' intuitive thinking. However, thinking is the most complex spiritual phenomenon of human beings. In the process of thinking, the forms of logical intuition and image often work seamlessly and alternately. You have me and I have you, which are inseparable, and more importantly, they cannot be completely separated.

In the process of reading "Sherlock Holmes," I will introduce some knowledge about intuitive thinking, and talk about my personal experience. It is inevitable that there are superficial and fallacies, and I sincerely hope that readers will criticize and give advice.

Let's briefly understand what is intuitive thinking?

The original meaning of the word "intuition" in Latin is to stare and watch intently; in English and German, it has the meaning of observation and watching, mainly referring to directly perceiving or grasping the truth. The word "intuition" first appeared in our country was in modern times. It can be seen in Lu Xun's *Lace Literature·Reckoning*": "But I feel intuitively that this is probably a loss,..." But this does not mean that there was no concept similar to intuition in ancient China, and no writings about intuition. "Chuai" and "Mo" in *Guiguzi* during the Warring States period BC have the connotation of intuition, "Chapter Chuai" and "Chapter Mo" are special statements about intuition.

Since Qian Xuesen proposed to establish the discipline of thinking science in the 1980s, the discussion of intuition has become a noticeable topic in the domestic research fields of philosophy, psychology, scientific methodology and so on. Many researchers and enthusiasts have flooded with ideas and launched a large number of insightful papers and works. Due to the complexity of intuition itself and other objective reasons, many problems have not been thoroughly studied, and even the definition has not reached a complete consensus. In this sense, intuitive thinking is the youngest form of thinking. But in general, regarding intuition, the more inclined views are: one, it is carried out on the basis of experience and knowledge; two, it is random and sudden; three, it is illogical. Its definition can be expressed as a form of thinking that is based on the existing knowledge, experience and factual clues, and quickly sees, penetrates, and grasps the regularity and essential characteristics of the thinking object.

Intuitive thinking is one of the thinking forms as important as logical thinking and image thinking.*General Psychology* defines intuitive thinking as a thinking activity that people can quickly understand and make judgments when facing new problems, new things and phenomena.Bruner believes that intuition is "smart speculation, rich assumptions and bold and quick to make experimental conclusions".Dong Qi defines intuitive thinking as "a thinking process in which the human brain, based on limited data and facts, mobilizes all existing knowledge and experience to make rapid identification, keen insight, direct understanding and overall judgment of the nature and regular connection of objective things".Intuition investigation thinking was put forward by Wang Fuxiang in 1999. He believed that the main body of investigation, based on the existing knowledge and experience, jumped from the whole to directly and quickly grasp the essence of criminal cases.It can be seen from this that intuition investigation thinking refers to the thinking form in which the investigation subject quickly perceives, identifies and wholly grasps the regularity and essential characteristics of the thinking object on the basis of the existing knowledge, experience and fact clues in the specific field of investigation and the whole process of investigation.In other words, it is the operation and reflection of intuitive thinking in the whole investigation process.

Intuitive thinking, logical thinking and image thinking are the three most recognized forms of thinking. Logical thinking uses abstract concepts as raw materials for reasoning and judgment. The thinking process is rigorous and meticulous, and the conclusions are accurate and reliable. However, it has higher requirements for raw materials, namely concepts, as well as the closed and single process of the whole process, and the pursuit of the certainty of right and wrong, and true and false, which sometimes inevitably leads thinking into dilemma. Image thinking is a kind of logical thinking based on image, such as human expression, action, emotion (happiness, anger, sorrow, likes and dislikes), image vocabulary, color, lines, notes, etc. The process of image thinking is relatively open, and the conclusion is vivid.

The raw materials of intuitive thinking cover the above two, which can be concrete images of various objects in nature, or scientific concepts and symbols that express scientific connotations. That is to say, all kinds of thinking materials are inclusive, and no thinking materials will be rejected. However, in general, the raw materials of intuitive thinking are more inclined to current things, phenomena, and problems to be solved. The accuracy of intuitive thinking is not as good as that of logical thinking, and it is necessary to constantly confirm or revise with new information or facts, or even carry out logical arguments, in order to become a definite conclusion. The biggest difference between intuitive thinking and logical thinking and image thinking is that the former is a form of thinking that instantly cuts in and obtains a conclusion, while the latter two are forms of thinking that operate according to a certain program and then obtain results.

Logical thinking is like a straight line that runs through it without branches or branches; image thinking is like a sine wave, with yin and yang, round and short, alternating with each other; intuitive thinking is like an irregular sawtooth wave, containing but not revealing, revealing but not floating. They each have their own merits, perform their own duties, and complement each other perfectly. Each of them can bloom brilliant flowers of thinking and bear the desired fruits of thinking.

In the inner "module" of intuition (to borrow computer terminology), there is a form that opens up and goes straight to the point, which is the momentary confident determination of the insight and overall grasp of the thinking object. It often appears in the form of unequivocal, indisputable affirmations and judgments. This is the conclusion type, that is, A=B. It is more typical in intuitive thinking, more active and more common. One of its features is that it is very fast. As Holmes said when he first saw Watson, "You have been in Afghanistan, I perceive." "The whole train of thought did not occupy a second." Watson was amazed at the speed and accuracy of the process. The second feature is full of confidence and straightforward. As Holmes said after inspecting the scene: "There has been murder done, and the murderer was a man. He was more than six feet high, was in the prime of life." "I am almost certain that this address has been written in a hotel."

The conclusion type is the affirmation or negation in tone and form, not the substantive conclusion. Despite the certainty in tone, there is no doubt that until the final result comes, its essence is speculation, guess and reckoning (described below).

Conclusive intuition must be "fast" and "accurate in judgment", and cannot be innate or acquired without learning. The sharpness of the sword is caused by sharpening, and the experience of Sherlock Holmes is very telling, which will be continuously introduced later. The conclusion type also has great defects, that is, the error rate is often relatively high, which requires us to be like Holmes. First, we should constantly confirm with new facts or conduct retrospective reasoning, and correct in time; second, we should strive to hone our observation—intuition ability. Only in this way can we effectively improve the accuracy of intuition.

B. Understanding of Sherlock Holmes' Expression and Speculation

In his "The Book of Life," Holmes claimed by a momentary expression, a twitch of a muscle or a glance of an eye, to fathom a man's inmost thoughts.

Watson commented:Deceit, according to him, was an impossibility in the case of one trained to observation and analysis. His conclusions were as infallible as so many propositions of Euclid. So startling would his results appear to the uninitiated that until they learned the processes by which he had arrived at them they might well consider him as a necromancer.

From this, it can be considered that Sherlock Holmes was probably the first detective to study micro-expressions and micro-motions.

First of all, let's see whether Holmes' instantaneous expression and muscles (mainly referring to the face; eyes and the look of eyes will be introduced later) about a person hide thoughts.

An American psychologist has a formula, the result of information exchange=7% speech+38% intonation and speed+55% expression and action. Expression and action account for more than half of the total, and the total amount of nonverbals accounts for 93%.

Some researchers divide human facial expressions into three types. One is slight expressions: the entire facial muscles are almost involved, but the intensity is not large. The second is local expression: some muscles are involved. The third is micro-expressions: expressions that are fleeting but can express feelings, the time may be half a second or even less.

Studies have found that there are more than 40 muscles in the human face, most of which we cannot consciously control, and our reaction speed is faster than our thinking.

Therefore, facial expressions reveal a lot of information unconsciously. But many people can't interpret it correctly. After in-depth research, the researchers also found some relatively recognized emoticons that can be used for reference.

There are mainly seven types of recognized human expression packs, each of which expresses a different meaning.

Happy: facial actions include turning up the corners of the mouth, lifting and wrinkling the cheeks, shrinking the eyelids, and forming "crow's feet" at the end of the eyes.

Sad: facial features include squinting, eyebrows tightened, corners of the mouth pulled down, chin raised or tightened.

Fear: mouth and eyes open, eyebrows raised, nostrils widened.

Anger: brows drooping, forehead wrinkled, eyelids and lips tense.

Disgust: sniffling, upper lip raised, eyebrows drooping, eyes squinting.

Surprised: jaw drooping, lips and mouth relaxed, eyes wide open, lids and eyebrows slightly raised.

Contempt: one side of the mouth is raised in a sneer or smirk.

It can be seen that there is a certain physiological and psychological basis for Sherlock Holmes to discover the traces of people's mentality through people's facial expressions and muscles.

Secondly, let's take a look at how to discover the hidden rich connotations of people's faces and muscles.

As mentioned above, different thinking forms have certain selectivity for different information sources. People's expressions and muscle changes, these lively and immediate information are one of the most "loving" thinking materials for intuition. In particular, what Sherlock Holmes asked was to "infer the innermost thoughts" from people's "instant" expressions and muscles, so as to be "predictable". This inevitably requires a high degree of sensitivity and insight in thinking, in order to capture the seemingly ordinary but actually unusual things through the instantaneous changes of people's external expressions and muscles. This characteristic is peculiar to intuitive thinking. This ability is especially important for detectives.

In other words, the connotation of people's "instant" expression and muscle changes is mainly learned through "speculation".

Speculate, means to measure the unknown according to the known; conjecture, means to speculate and estimate; guess also means to speculate and conjecture. They are basically synonymous.

In the "module" of intuitive thinking, another form is called speculative type, also known as conjecturing type and guessing type, which often appears in the posture of being unpredictable and predicting things like God, that is, X = A ?. The speculative type is a speculative (conjecturing, guessing) conclusion based on limited and uncertain phenomena, clues and other known information.Holmes had a lot of speculation, conjecture and guess (basically synonymous with speculation) in the process of investigation.His extraordinary level of speculation pointed out the right direction for his smooth investigation of the case.As the former Soviet Union criminal investigation expert Berkin said in his *A New Probe into the World's Strange Cases*, experienced investigators sometimes make correct **guesses** based on trivial evidence, some non substantive plots in the case and the details of the suspect's behavior. This phenomenon is called detective intuition.That is to say, the detection of intuition or intuitive detection is actually the operation of the thinking phenomenon of guessing (or speculating, conjecturing) in the detection work. That is to say, guessing (speculating, conjecturing) is one of the basic functions of intuition and the normal state of intuitive thinking. When the thinking subject thinks that it has certainty and evidence and is confident that the "guess" is correct, it will directly point to the conclusion in an unquestionable tone. This is the conclusion type described earlier. If you find that there is a problem and you can't "guess" the result temporarily, you will be suspicious and need to be confirmed. This is the suspicious type in the intuition module. After thinking and "guessing" for a long time, the revelation suddenly obtained is the epiphany type (also called the sudden awakening type), which is a special form of intuition. These two types are described later. That is to say, conclusion type, speculation type, doubt type and epiphany type are the main performance modes of intuitive thinking.

C. Understanding of Sherlock Holmes' Cultivation of Observation Ability

Holmes said in his "The Book of Life": "If a person who is good at observation makes accurate and systematic observation of the things he touches, he will have a great harvest." This sentence used two "observations" in succession, indicating that Holmes attached great importance to observation.

Holmes believed that beginners (observers) might as well start with simpler problems. For example, when you meet a person, you have to **recognize** the person's experience and occupation **at a glance**. Such training can sharpen one's ability to observe. We also have to learn how to observe people and what to look at. For example, a person's fingernails, sleeves, boots, the knees of trousers, calluses between the thumb and index finger, facial expressions, shirt cuffs, etc., can all reveal his occupation.

However, the ability to "discern" this "**at a glance**" is difficult to obtain by relying on observation alone. Especially when we want to "study difficult problems such as moral and psychological problems", we have to rely on intuitive thinking, which is powerful and penetrating, because only intuitive thinking has this unique function.

D. Understanding of Holmes' "I have a turn both for observation and for deduction":

Holmes said, "I have a turn both for observation and for deduction."(17)

Observation, a purposeful and planned perceptual behavior, is an advanced form of perception.Observation refers to perception behaviors such as seeing, listening, touching and modeling. Observation is to analyze, think and see the essence. That is to say, observation is not only a simple perception process, but also includes other perception and thinking activities through the perception process, especially the visual process. This thinking activity includes logical thinking (reasoning), image thinking, and of course, intuitive thinking (insight, grasp).Intuitive thinking is naturally closely related to the visual system. Observation is a stepping stone. Intuitive thinking is the first thing touched by the results of observation.From the context of Sherlock Holmes' "The Book of Life," observation should include intuitive thinking, that is, "observation——intuition". Therefore, Holmes proudly said, "Observation with me is second nature" and confidently believed that "I have a kind of intuition that way".

Holmes had an explanation for his intuition. He boasted that he was the only "consulting detective" in the world. There were many official and private detectives in London. When they met difficulties, they would go to him to guide them. Almost all of them could get satisfactory results.

In Watson's words, "Do you mean to say that without leaving your room you can unravel some knot which other men can make nothing of, although they have seen every detail for themselves?" The mysterious function of this Sherlock Holmes believed that it was his outstanding intuitive thinking.If you don't believe it, you can hear how Holmes answered Watson: "Quite so.I have a kind of intuition that way.Now and again a case turns up which is a little more complex. Then I have to bustle about and seeing things with my own eyes." That is to say, Holmes could let his clients find clues in the foggy cases and solve the cases by sitting on the sofa in Baker Street and listening to the case introduction. Only those cases that were slightly complicated needed him to go to the scene personally to find problems and solve them.

It can be seen that although intuitive thinking prefers current and fresh information, it will never ignore "second-hand" and indirect information. This is determined by the well-established mechanism of intuitive thinking.

E. Holmes' Comparison of Intuition and Reasoning:

"It was easier to know it than to explain why I know it.If you are asked to prove that two and two make four, you might find some difficulty, and yet you are quite sure of the fact." Holmes made a very simple and appropriate explanation of the expression process of intuition and reasoning. You "see"——that is, it is easy to intuitively get the result. However, if you want to explain the origin of the result, you must carry out logical reasoning, which takes a lot of words. This is just like everyone knows that 2 plus 2 equals 4, not 3 or 5.

F. Sherlock Holmes' Intuition Show (No.2)

"I wonder what that fellow is looking for?" Watson asked, pointing to a stalwart, plainly dressed individual who was walking slowly down the other side of the street, looking anxiously at the numbers.He had a large blue envelope in his hand, and was evidently the bearer of a message.

"You mean the retired sergeant of Marines, "said Holmes.

Watson thought to himself that Holmes was bragging! "He knows that I cannot verify his guess." At that moment, there came a knock and a talk. It was the postman who delivered the letter to Holmes. The opportunity had come! Watson wanted to take this opportunity to frustrate Holmes' arrogance and prevent him from making false statements. He asked the postman what he had done before. When Watson heard the same answer as Holmes' "guess", he was hooded.It can be seen from this that when the final result is not reached, the conclusion type is still a guess in essence, a guess with full assurance and confidence.

Watson asked Holmes, "How in the world did you deduce that?"

Holmes reasoned, "Even across the street I could see a great blue anchor tattooed on the back of the fellow's hand. That smacked of the sea.He had a military carriage, however, and regulation side whiskers.There we have the marine.He was a man with some amount of self-importance and a certain air of command.You must have observed the way in which he held his head and swung his cane.A steady, respectble, middle-aged man, too, on the face of him—all facts which lead me to believe that he had been a sergeant."

If Holmes believed that Watson had been to Afghanistan at a glance, Watson was surprised, and thought that Holmes was secretive and even secretly investigated him; If Watson saw Holmes' theory of observation intuition in "The Book of Life" and thought it was an unpredictability and fantasy, then when he heard that Holmes could say that the postman across the street was a "retired sergeant of Marines", he could not help showing "surprise and admiration".

G. Holmes' Intuitive Investigation after Investigating the Scene:

One day, Holmes received a letter from Officer Gregson, saying that a murder had occurred at 3 Lauriston Gardens off the Brixton Road. There was a man's body in it. He was well dressed. There was neither evidence of robbery nor any evidence that could explain the cause of death. Although there were several bloodstains in the house, there was no scar on the deceased. They were puzzled by how the deceased entered the empty house and felt that the case was extremely difficult. It was hoped that Holmes would be here before 12:00. Holmes and Watson hurried to the crime scene by hansom. One hundred yards from the scene, they got off the carriage and carefully observed the surrounding buildings and roads from far to near before entering the room. According to the investigation of the crime scene, Holmes launched his rich and agile thinking wings.

1. Psychological portrait of the criminal (intuitive results in front, reasoning or explanation behind):
   ① It is a murder case (conclusive): this is certain, but it is not sure whether it is political murder, money killing or love killing.
   ② It is a man (conclusion type): it can be seen from the stride and leather shoe print.
   ③ Height more than six feet (guessing type): judging from the stride and the words on the wall six feet above the ground.
   ④ It is the prime of life (conclusion type): "Well, if a man can stride four and half feet without the smallest effort, he can't be quite in sere and yellow. That was the breadth of a puddle on the garden walk which he had evidently walked across. Patent-leather boots had gone round and Square-toes had hopped over."
   ⑤ Feet are a little smaller than the figure (speculative type): it can be seen from the proportion of stride and shoe print.
   ⑥ One is tall and the other is short (conclusion type): "That was the breadth of a puddle on the garden walk which he had evidently walked across. Patent-leather boots had gone round and Square-toes had hopped over." "In this way my second link was formed, which told me that the nocturnal visitors were two in number, one remarkable for his height(as I calculated from the length of his stride), and the other fashionably dressed, to judge from the small and elegant impression left by his boots."

⑦ The tall man is the killer (conclusion type): "The tall one, then, had done the murder, if murder there was."

⑧ It's a Trichinopoly cigar (conclusion type): "I gathered up some scattered ash from the floor.It was dark in colour and flaky——such an ash is only made by a Trichinopoly.I have made a special study of cigar ashes——in fact, I have written a monograph on the subject.I flatter myself that I can distinguish at a glance the ash of any known brand either of cigar or of tobacco."

"The very first thing which I observed on arriving there was that a cab had made two ruts with its wheels close to the curb.Now, up to last night, we have had no rain for a week, so that those wheels which left such a deep impression must have been there during the night.There were the marks of the horse's hoofs, too, the outline of one of which was far more clearly cut than that of the other three, showing that was a new shoe.Since the cab was there after the rain began, and was not there at any time during the morning——I have Gregson's word for that——it follows that it must have been there during the night, and, therefore, that it brought those two individuals to the house."

⑩ He is a ruddy-faced man(speculation type): "I had already come to the conclusion, since there were no signs of a struggle, that the blood which covered the floor had burst from the murder's nose in his excitement.I could perceive that the track of blood coincided with the track of his feet.It is seldom that any man, unless he is very full-blooded, breaks out in this way through emotions, so I hazarded the opinion that the criminal was probably a robust and ruddy-faced man.Events proved that I had judged correctly."

⑪ The nail on the right hand is noticeably long (conclusion type): "The writing on the wall was done with a man's forefinger dipped in blood.My glass allowed me to observe that the plaster was slightly scratched in doing it, which would not have been the case if the man's nail had been trimmed."

Thinking is one of the most complex spiritual phenomena of human beings. If we carefully decompose it, we will find that many modules will appear alternately in the operation of intuition.

The psychological portrait is mostly seen in the speculation type, because the background of the object is complex, the materials are scarce and limited, and the outcome has not yet been finalized. The process of moving towards the outcome is full of variables. Many complex situations need to be further verified. The thinking subject naturally has little grasp and lacks confidence.Because Holmes is straightforward and intuitive, there are more conclusion types with bold tone and full confidence in his works. Generally speaking, the conclusion type appears more in simple cases and events, and the results can be seen immediately. For example, Holmes said to Watson "You have been in Afghanistan, I perceive" and said that the identity of the postman across the street was a "retired sergeant of Marines".

2. **Intuitive conclusions about the "wedding ring", the cause of death of the victim and German:**

① The appearance of "wedding ring" makes the motive of murder point to love killing.

When the victim's body was lifted, a ring fell on the floor. Lestrade quickly picked it up and stared at it in bewilderment. "There is been a woman here," He cried, "It's a woman's wedding ring."

"This complicates matters," said Gregson. "Heaven knows, they were complicated enough before."

"You're sure it doesn't simplify them? "observed Holmes. If Holmes has not formed a clear direction in the political murder, money killing and love killing before, then it can be basically inferred as the latter - love killing.

② The victim was poisoned by poison:

"If this man was murdered, how was it done?" asked Lestrade.

"Poison," said Holmes definitely.

Watson said of Holmes, "The more I thought of it the more extraordinarily did my companion's hypothesis, that the man had been poisoned, appear."

Why did the victim die by taking "poison"? Holmes later added, "Having sniffed the dead man's lips, I detected a slightly sour smell..."

At the same time, Holmes further affirmed that "he had had poison forced upon him".

Holmes reasoned and speculated as follows:

"There was no wound on the dead man's person, but the agitated expression upon his face assured me that he had foreseen his fate before it came upon him. Men who die from heart disease, or any sudden natural cause, never by any chance exhibit agitation upon their features....I came to the conclusion that he had poison forced upon him.Again, I argued that it had been forced upon him from the hatred and fear expressed upon his face."

③ Is it an intuitive conclusion that "rache" is "revenge"?

Holmes said: "'Rache,' is the German for 'revenge'..." Is this judgment an intuitive conclusion? We can say no, we can also say yes.

We can say no.The perpetrator later explained that the reason for this prank was: "I remember a German being found in New York with RACHE written up above him, and it was argued at the time in the newspapers that the secret societies must have done it.I guessed that what puzzled the New Yorkers would would puzzle the Londoners, so I dipped my finger in my own blood and printed in on a convenient place on the wall. "Although the work does not write whether Holmes knew about the case in New York, the work said that Holmes, "He appears to know all every detail of every horror perpetrated in the century."

We can also say yes.Because the work does not write whether Holmes knows German, but it is likely that he has a certain understanding of the German structure or writing methods to make intuitive judgments.So Holmes is sure: "...it was simply a blind intended to put the police upon a wrong track, by suggesting Socialism and secret societies.It was not done by a German.The A, if you noticed, was printed somewhat after the German fashion.Now, a real German invariably prints in the Latin character, so that we may safely say that this was not written by one, but by a clumsy imitator who overdid his part.It was simply a ruse to divert inquiry into a wrong channel." It is more in line with the author's original intention to make an intuitive judgment, and it is also conducive to the shaping of Holmes' "magical detective" image.

H. Holmes' general speculation about the whole case:

Holmes left the scene and went to the post office to send a telegram to Cleveland police station to investigate the background information of the deceased when he went to find Rance, the first police officer who found the scene of the case. Then he said to Watson with confidence: "...as a matter of fact, my mind is entirely made up upon the case, but still we may as well learn all that is to be learned."

Why was Holmes so sure? Because after the first-hand information from the investigation of the crime scene, he had formed the speculative investigation idea of "ring——coachman——murderer" in his mind. Then he decided to look for the murderer from the ring.

Of course, whether the overall speculation of the whole case is correct or not needs to be supported by evidence in the investigation, as Holmes said: "There is nothing like first-hand evidence." The result finally proved that Holmes' overall speculation on the whole case was correct.

I. Holmes' intuitive reaction when he asked constable Rance:

In order to master the first-hand case, Holmes asked Rance, the constable on the night of the crime.

Rance described the situation at that time in detail:My time is from ten at night to six in the morning.At eleven there was a fight at the White Hart;but bar that was quiet enough on the beat.At one o'clock it began to rain, and I met Harry Murcher—him who has the Holland Grove beat—and we stood together at the corner of Henrietta Street a-talkin'.Presently—maybe about two or a little after—I thought I would take a look round and see that all was right down the Brixson Road.It was precious dirty and lonely.Not a soul did I meet all the way down, though a cab or two went past me.It was a-strollin' down, thinkin' between ourselves how uncommon handy a four of gin hot would be, when suddenly the glint of a light caught my eye in the window of that same house.Now, I knew that them two houses in Lauriston Gardens was empty on account of him that owns them who won't have the drains seed to, though the very last tenant what lived in one of them died o'typhoid fever.I was knocked all in a heap, therefore, at seeing a light in the window, and I suspected as something was wrong.When I got to the door—

"You stopped, and then walked back to the garden gate," Holmes interrupted. "What did you do that for?" —Sherlock Holmes speculated according to the on-site investigation and Rance's description.

Rance gave a violent jump, and stared at Holmes with the utmost amazement upon his features.

"Why, that's true, sir," he said:Though how you come to know it, Heaven only knows. You see when I got up to the door, it was so still and so lonesome, that I thought I'd be none the worse for someone with me.I looked to see if I could see Murcher's lantern, but there wasn't no sign of him nor of anyone else.Then I pulled myself together and went back and pushed the door open.All was quiet inside, so I went into the room where the light a-burnin'.There was a candle flickerin' on the mantelpiece———a red wax one——— and by its light I saw———

"You walked around the room for several times, knelt down beside the dead body, and then walked over to push the kitchen door. Later -" Holmes continued to speculate in a positive tone based on the scene investigation and what Rance said.

John Rance sprang to his feet with a frightened face and suspicion in his eyes. "Where was you hid to see all that?" he cried. "It seems to me that you knows a deal more than you should."

Holmes laughed and threw his card across the table to the constable."Don't go arresting me for the murder," he said. "I am one of the hounds and not the wolf; Mr. Gregson or Mr. Lestrade will answer for that. Go on, though. What did you do next?"

Rance resumed his seat, without, however, losing his mystified expression.

"I went back to the gate and sounded my whistle. That brought Murcher and two more to the spot."

"Was the street empty then?" asked Holmes.Rance said that he only saw a drunken man standing at the door, leaning against the railing, raising his voice and singing a tune loudly.

"What sort of a man was he?" asked Holmes."His face–his dress–didn't you notice them?" Holmes broke in impatiently.

"I should think I did notice them, seeing that I had to prop him up–me and Murcher between us. He was a long chap, with a red face, the lower part muffled round– –"

"That will do," cried Holmes. "What became of him?""How was he dressed?"——— Holmes speculated that the man was the murderer.

"A brown overcoat."

"Had he a whip in his hand?"

"A whip–no."

"He must have left it behind," muttered Holmes.———According to the scene investigation and Rance's description, Holmes could be absolutely sure that the drunk who slipped away from Rance's eyes was the criminal.

J. Holmes' intuition on the ring:

1. Can a ring be used as bait to catch criminals?

Watson asked, could the criminal come with the ring as bait as promised? Holmes' answer was very positive.Holmes explained, "...this man would rather risk anything than lose the ring." Because this ring had a special meaning, he even arbitrarily thought: "You shall see him within an hour." This, of course, is what the author did to beautify and deify Holmes' bold and forthright personality and outstanding intuition. However, he was not sure whether the criminal had come in person, and then added: "If he does not come himself, he will send an accomplice." It illustrates Holmes' ability and sophistication.

2. Speculation on the loss of the ring:

Holmes said: "According to my notion he dropped it while stooping over Drebber's body, and did not miss it at the time. After leaving the house he discovered his loss and hurried back, but found the police already in possession, owing to his own folly in leaving the candle burning. He had to pretend to be drunk in order to allay the suspicions which might have been aroused by his appearance at the gate." Holmes' conjecture was reasonable and accurately reproduced the scene of the criminal at that time.

K. The investigation results confirm the intuitive judgment of love killing:

Holmes' investigation of the background of the perpetrator confirmed his intuitive judgment that the motive of the murder was a love killing case: "I have just had an answer to my American telegram. My view of the case is the correct one."

Holmes backtracked: "Having left the house, I proceeded to do what Gregson had neglected.I telegraphed to the head of the police at Cleveland, limiting my inquiry to the circumstances connected with the marriage of Enoch Drebber. The answer was conclusive. It told me that Drebber had already applied for the protection of the law against an old rival in love, named Jefferson Hope, and that this same Hope was at present in Europe. I knew now that I held the clue to the mystery in my hand, and all that remained was to secure the murderer.I knew at that time that I had the clue of this secret case, and all I had to do was catch the murderer." That is to say, Holmes had not only determined (conclusive, the same below) that it was a love killing case, but also determined that the murderer was Hope.

L. Holmes' guess about the scene of Stan Jason's murder:

Lestrade told about his investigation process and found that Stangerson was also assassinated. "And now comes the strangest part of the affair. What do you suppose was above the murdered man?" asked Lestrade.

"The word RACHE, written in letters of blood," Holmes said.Holmes said, "It's Rachel, written in blood."——Holmes guessed right. In fact, he had already "guessed" from the development of a series of cases, and similar blood characters might appear on the wall. At this moment, Lestrade seemed to be in a fog.

"That was it," said Lestrade, in an awestruck voice.

M. Holmes' inference about the murder scene of Stangerson:

Lestrade told the story of Stangerson's experience at the murder scene of the hotel. He said that a child saw someone climbing down the ladder from an open window on the third floor at the back of the hotel. The child remembered him as a tall man with a red face and a long brown coat.When he heard that the description of this man was completely consistent with Holmes' inference of the murderer, Watson glanced at him, but his face did not show any complacency—Holmes' speculation was strengthened.

Holmes asked about the leftovers at the scene. When Lestrede said that there was a small chip ointment box containing a couple of pills, Holmes sprang from his chair with an exclamation of delight.

"The last link," he cried, exultantly. "My case is complete." Most of the materials in my hand are translated into "assertions"; Yu Fang, Huacheng Publishing House, translated it as "inference", which means the same thing and is the result of logical thinking. Ruiye, Nanhai Publishing House, compiles it as "I have straightened out all the clues". It does not involve specific thinking forms, but the process of straightening out must be through thinking. This thinking logic is OK, so is intuition. These translations are beyond reproach and conform to the original meaning. Of course, if the author translated it, it would be translated as "deduce": it is determined by the speculation made with great assurance that the poison used to kill Drebber was finally found, and the speculation that the poison would kill was established.

N. Holmes' epiphany:

Holmes speculated that the deadly thing of Drebber was poison, so he was interested in the pills that Lestrade found, so he decided to experiment on dogs. When half of the first pill did not respond, his face looked extremely upset and disappointed. He bit his lips and knocked on the table with his fingers, showing impatience. He suddenly realized: "Ah, I have it! I have it!" He quickly took out the other one, cut it in half, then dissolved it in water and milk, and put it in front of the dog. The small animal even died before its tongue was completely wet. Holmes finally breathed a long sigh.

Holmes has already mentioned this phenomenon in his "The Book of Life." He said that the cultivation of observation ability should be carried out from every aspect and every detail of a person. "That all united should fail to enlighten the competent inquirer in any case is almost inconceivable." This "sudden understanding" refers to intuitive insight.

Epiphany, also known as sudden awareness, is a special form of intuition, that is, A...→B. Originally from the Buddhist term, it refers to sudden comprehension. Intuitive epiphany is an extended meaning, which refers to a sudden idea or plan, such as a flash of lightning, which is fleeting and can not be found. There are similarities and differences with inspiration. The same is the flower of thought that suddenly descends after thinking hard. The difference is that intuitive insight is mainly aimed at the solutions and ideas of problems, and the obtained conclusions are not necessarily correct; inspiration mainly occurs in literary and artistic creation and scientific research, and the results obtained are often more mature.

O. Holmes' intuition that the murderer is a groom:

"I had already determined in my own mind that the man who had walked into the house with Drebber was none other than the man who had driven the cab."

The following is the reasoning process of Holmes on this intuitive conclusion:

1. The marks in the road showed me that the horse had wandered on in a way which would have been impossible had there been anyone in charge of it.Where, then, could the driver be, unless he were inside the house?

2. Again, it is absurd to suppose that any sane man would carry out a deliberate crime under the very eyes, as it were, of a third person, who was sure to betray him.

3. Lastly, supposing one man wished to dog another through London, what better means could he adopt than to turn cabdriver?All these considerations led me to the irresistible conclusion that Jefferson Hope was to be found among the jarveys of the Metropolis.

4. If he had been one, there was no reason to believe that he had ceased to be. On the contrary, from his point of view, any sudden change would be likely to draw attention to himself. He would probably, for a time at least, continue to perform his duties.

5. There was no reason to suppose that he was going under an assumed name. Why should he change his name in a country where no one knew his original one?

I therefore organized my street Arab detective corps, and sent them systematically to every cab proprietor in London until they ferreted out the man that I wanted.

P. Watson's doubts:

When Holmes saw at a glance that he had returned from Afghanistan, he was very surprised, which inspired Watson's "curiosity" about Holmes:

First, he was curious about Holmes' interest and purpose of life. His interest in Holmes and his curiosity as to Holmes' aims in life gradually deepened and increased.

The second was the curiosity about Holmes' occupation and knowledge structure. Neither did he appear to have pursued any course of reading which might fit him for a degree in science or any other recognized portal which would give him an entrance into the learned world. Yet his zeal for certain studies was remarkable, and within eccentric limits his knowledge was so extraordinarily ample and minute that his observations have fairly astounded Watson. Holmes' ignorance was as remarkable as his knowledge.

Third, he was curious: His quiet, self-confident manner convinced Watson that he had already formed a theory which explained all the facts, though what it was Watson could not for an instant **conjecture**.

2. Watson's "strange idea" about the case:

As a bystander, Watson' mind had been too much excited by all that had occurred, and the strangest fancies and surmises crowded into it.

"The strangest fancies" and "surmises" are a way of thinking. To have doubts is to be puzzled and ponder over problems found.It is often the case that the thinking subject can not immediately reach a conclusion when facing the problems found, or the conclusion is in a hazy state, at this time, he has to hang up the question to find new evidence to solve the problem.The words "doubt", "strange", "curious", "abnormal" and other related phenomena that we usually speak of belong to a form of intuitive thinking—doubt type, that is, A=?. Watson's "surmises" about Holmes and "the strangest fancies" about the case are typical forms of intuitive doubt.

There are sometimes one or more pending doubts. One type of doubt is single doubt, which aims at relatively simple information sources. One doubt leads to another, or there are multiple doubts at the same time, which is called paranoia.When a series of or layers of questions accumulate more and more, people are more and more motivated to solve the mystery.For example, Watson's three overlapping "surmises" about Holmes drove him to explore Holmes. With the in-depth understanding of Holmes, Watson relieved his doubts and dispelled his original ideas.

Q. Lestrade's intuition:

On a rough yellow plaster wall at the scene, Police Officer Lestrade found two words scrawled in blood: RACHE, which he believed was a woman's name.

"And what does it mean now that you have found it?" asked Gregson in a depreciatory voice.

Lestrade said:"Mean? Why, it means that the writer was going to put the female name Rachel, but was disturbed before he or she had time to finish. You mark my words, when this case comes to be cleared up, you will find that a woman named Rachel has something to do with it." Is it true? Let's first understand Lestrade's cognitive process —direct perception.

Direct perception, although it presents many aspects of things, like a three-dimensional picture, it only reflects part or external attributes of the objective things. There is also an intuitive level below it. Intuition is the stage of human perception and the most direct and simple understanding and reflection of objective things.For example, at the scene of the crime, we saw a well-dressed man's corpse with several blood characters written on the corner. It was like a plane picture at a glance. This is the intuitive result. If we saw this scene through direct perception, a well-dressed man's corpse, with several blood characters written in the corner, the meaning of which sounds like a woman's name, we would draw a conclusion like Lestrade.When people meet for the first time, they can only remember their faces and faces, but know little about their deep contents; The salesperson of a clothing store can know the size of a customer's clothes by taking a glance at their body shape; The driver drives the vehicle to avoid various obstacles, which are the result of direct perception. Although direct perception can be seen at a glance, it does not have the ability to know the autumn with one leaf or understand the essence of things in small ways. What you see is basically the phenomenon of things, so you should not stay at this level and be satisfied with it.American neuroscientist Marcus Rekeley has been engaged in brain research for decades. He found that whenever a specific thinking task is completed, the brain will return to the default "dormant state", and the direct sense is basically in this "dormant state" or "sub thinking state". In other words, direct perception mainly wanders at the edge of perception and thinking. Therefore, it is not surprising to feel "like" catching up on rumours and making sense of them. If the investigation and case solving remain at this stage, it will mislead the direction of investigation, delay the fight, and even cause unjust and wrong cases.

Lestrade's simple and arbitrary conclusion of the blood word showed that his cognition was at the level of directness, which was superficial and incomprehensible. As a result, he was smitten by the facts and ridiculed by Holmes.

R. Gregson's intuition:

Gregson found the hat shop through the hat of the victim at the scene of the crime, and found the customer who bought the hat in the hat shop. It was Mr. Drebber, the victim, residing at Charpentier's Boarding Establishment, Torquay Terrace.So, Gregson first asked the landlady:

"I found her very pale and distressed. Her daughter was in the room, too–an uncommonly fine girl she is, too; she was looking red about the eyes and her lips trembled as I spoke to her. That didn't escape my notice. I began to smell a rat. You know the feeling, Mr. Sherlock Holmes, when you come upon the right scent–a kind of thrill in your nerves. 'Have you heard of the mysterious death of your late boarder Mr. Enoch J. Drebber, of Cleveland?' I asked."

"The mother nodded. She didn't seem able to get out a word. The daughter burst into tears. I felt more than ever that these people knew something of the matter."

Gregson was good at observing words and expressions. Their faces, expressions, eyes, lips and other details started his intuition, and it was right to speculate that they had secret feelings with the case and the victim. As a result, his interest increased sharply and he stepped forward step by step. He inquired about the landlady and finally found out the "criminal"—Arthur, the son of the landlady.

It turned out that during the three weeks of renting the house, Drebber, the tenant, not only behaved frivolously to the maids, but also often spoke disrespectfully to Alice, the beautiful landlady's daughter. Even his secretary, Stangerson, scolded Drebber for being inhuman.One day, Drebber came back from drinking and forced Alice away in front of the landlady, which angered Arthur, who was on vacation at home.He was a naval lieutenant. He had a short temper and loved his sister very much.There was yelling and scuffling at home, and they were in a mess. Later, they fought in the street. Then Arthur laughed at the door with a stick in his hand and said, "I don't think that fine fellow will trouble us again." The next morning, when they heard that Mr. Drebber had been murdered, the landlady and Alice guessed that Arthur might have done it, so they had an abnormal look and behavior.

According to the results of his inquiry, Gregson also speculated that the murderer of Drebber was Arthur, and because after catching Arthur, he would confess without being forced to say, "I suppose you are arresting me for being concerned in the death of that scoundrel Drebber." "We had said nothing to him about it, so that his alluding to it had a most suspicious aspect."

Arthur's statement of "self admission" strengthened Gregson's speculation about him. Obviously, Gregson had a problem in asking Arthur. He regarded coincidence as inevitable, preconceived, and his idea of presumption of guilt biased him.

Then, Gregson guessed the scene of Arthur's crime:

"Well, my theory is that he followed Drebber as far as the Brixton Road. When there, a fresh altercation arose between them, in the course of which Drebber received a blow from the stick, in the pit of the stomach perhaps, which killed him without leaving any mark. The night was so wet that no one was about, so Charpentier dragged the body of his victim into the empty house." The facts after the case was solved proved that Gregson's conjecture was not consistent with the facts of the case, which was completely subjective. Gregson's intuitive judgment of Arthur's actions was inaccurate, which ultimately led to a serious deviation in the direction of investigation.

From a large number of cases, we can see that the most significant characteristics of intuitive thinking——

The first is "fast", that is, "be triggered at any moment" (most of them are conclusion type). The results can be obtained directly without complicated reasoning process.

The second is "sharp", that is, "penetrating insight", which can find bumps on the seemingly flat road and wonders in the seemingly ordinary scenery (most of them are suspicious).

The third is "obstinacy", that is, "being arrogant and unruly". The thinking process will not be in line with the rules, and will often be able to survive in times of adversity (mainly speculation and insight).

If logical thinking is likened to a girl who keeps herself quiet like a virgin, then intuitive thinking is like a boy who is naughty and unruly and moves like a rabbit. Although intuitive thinking has its outstanding advantages, if it is not mastered and used well, it is prone to deviation or even go astray.

Lestrade's inquiry into the landlady had entered the intuitive level through observation, but serious inaccuracy and deviation had occurred. In addition, he had a preconceived view of Arthur and believed his confession easily, which led to the wrong direction of investigation, resulting in the wrong arrest, and harming the innocent. This is a "hard wound" to intuition.

Inaccurate intuition will bring a lot of negative energy to people. Many misunderstandings, preconceptions, contradictions and even conflicts between people, even between organizations, political parties and countries, are often caused by the two sides' shadowy "suspicions", unrealistic "conjectures" and subjective arbitrary "conclusions" under the condition of asymmetric information.

So, how to heal the "wounds" of intuition, reduce and avoid the deviation or error of intuition?

First, think twice before you act. Intuitive thinking is accompanied by strong self-confidence from time to time after getting the conclusion. It is easy to have a whim. At this time, arbitrary and conceited emotions are most likely to occur. If we do not pay attention to absorbing new information and revising and enriching the conclusions, we can imagine the consequences once we take action.When Gregson speculated that the landlady and her daughter might be the insiders of the case through observation, he told Holmes how he felt: "You know the feeling, Mr. Sherlock Holmes, when you come upon the right scent–a kind of thrill in your nerves." A very sure guess is a conclusion (positive) type. This kind of self feeling is better after getting positive conclusions. It is easy to get carried away by the conclusion that "truth" is readily available.Therefore, when an intuitive result is produced, no matter the conclusion type or the doubt type, the speculation type or the insight type, do not put it into practice first, and try to put it aside for cold treatment. Generally speaking, the longer the time, the better. The cooling process is actually a process of inspection and correction. After this process, the correct rate is relatively high when we still firmly believe this conclusion.Stangerson was murdered in the hotel. A child saw a tall, red faced man in a long brown coat behind the hotel. He climbed down the ladder from an open window on the third floor.This man was exactly the same as the murderer Sherlock Holmes inferred, but his face did not show any complacency. It shows the great detective's calm and rational psychological quality.

Second, the verification is sufficient.The intuitive results can be tested on each "module" to see if there is any bias. In particular, the results obtained by the conclusion type are hasty and the accuracy rate is low. We might as well use the doubt type or the conjecture type to test; Similarly, speculative results can also be verified with conclusive or doubtful results. Of course, logical argumentation can also be carried out. The conclusion after such operation is more reliable.After Holmes left the scene of the crime at No. 3, Lauriston Gardens, he said to Watson: "as a matter of fact, my mind is entirely made up upon the case, but still we may as well learn all that is to be learned." "There is nothing like first-hand evidence." This fully shows that Holmes attaches great importance to the verification work.

Third, jump out of self-restraint.Intuitive thinking especially likes to take the self as the center to examine the world and draw the conclusion of "being self righteous". This is caused by the mechanism of intuitive thinking. Therefore, intuition comes from life, and we should see the essence through the phenomenon. Only by rebirth and nirvana can we reach the dialectical level.

Dialectical intuition is the highest realm of intuitive thinking and the sublimation of intuitive thinking. It leaps out of the confusion caused by the defects of intuition itself (to be introduced later). Those who are experienced can often grasp and apply dialectical intuitive thinking with ease.Sherlock Holmes, who enjoys high reputation, can undoubtedly be called a model—of course, dialectical intuition has also made Sherlock Holmes a magical detective.

2. The country of the Saints

S. About "Backtracking Reasoning":

The author used three "retrospective reasoning" when revealing the case through Holmes in the "end", which is a general procedure for intuitive thinking to explain "why" after obtaining the results. If there is no need to explain "why", retrospective reasoning will not occur, and reasoning masters will "have nothing to do". The relationship between intuition and retrospective reasoning is that the former is in the forefront, while the latter is closely followed by the aftermath, just like the sunny side of a mountain and the shady side of a team.

THE SIGN OF FOUR

1. Deductive method

A. Understanding of Holmes' "ideal detective":

HOLMES COMMENTED ON THE FAMOUS FRENCH DETECTIVE FRANCOIS LE VILLARD: "HE HAS all the Celtic power of quick intuition."

From this, we can draw a question: Is there any relationship between region and race and intuitive thinking? In other words, whether there are differences in their intuitive thinking ability in different regions and races. The answer is yes. The race and region are inseparable, which is just the so-called "one side of the land supports one side of the people". From the perspective of China, which has a vast territory and a large population of the same race, we can find some facts more or less. I don't have Holmes' boldness and insight, and I dare not label specific regions or ethnic groups. However, different regions or ethnic groups seem to breed such types of intuition as sensitivity, composure, laziness and slowness. The threshold of sensitive intuition is very low, as if there is an invisible intuition field all the time (special introduction later); calm intuition is neither humble nor arrogant, neither urgent nor slow, relatively rough and crazy; lazy intuition, lack of initiative and initiative, content with the status quo; Slow intuition makes everything slow, even dim.

When talking about the conditions needed to be an excellent detective, Holmes said of Francois Le Villard, "He has considerable gifts himself. He possesses two out of the three qualities necessary for the ideal detective. He has the power of observation and that of deduction. He is only wanting in knowledge, and that may come in time."

We can understand that observation (including intuition) and deduction are the weapons and souls of Holmes in all his investigations.

The third condition of Sherlock Holmes' ideal detective requires a "generalist" with extensive knowledge. This is also an important basis for generating intuition, which will be described in detail later.

B. Holmes' Intuition Show (No. 3):

Holmes said to Watson, "For example, observation shows me that you have been to the Wigmore Street Post-Office this morning, but deduction lets me know that when there you dispatched a telegram."

If it is transformed into a typical intuitive sentence pattern, it is: "You went to the Wigmore Street Office this morning". "How do you know?" "I know it by observation"; "You sent a telegram there", "How did you know?" "I got it by deduction".

Deduction is determined by Inference and belongs to the type of speculation. This raises the question of whether the "explanation" that follows the intuition show must be reasoning? The answer is not necessarily, it depends on the specific situation. Multipurpose reasoning for those who are more confident or whose information is more certain. In other words, if the basis of reasoning is relatively solid and certain, reasoning should be carried out. Because reasoning requires relatively high requirements for raw materials, of course, the conclusions are also relatively accurate. Such as the intuition show (1) (2) in "The Study of Blood Characters"; For those who are not sure or whose information is not very certain, use more speculation, speculation, estimates, and possibilities to speculate. "Because intuition does not require very high levels of raw materials, a few words or nuances can be used.". Of course, accuracy depends on the intuitive power of the thinking subject. In other words, after the intuition show, there will be a situation where reasoning and speculation go hand in hand and proceed alternately. The human mind is the most complex mental phenomenon. It has certain patterns and rules, but it is not rigidly bound by them. Adapting to circumstances and playing on the spot is the soul of thinking.

"Right!" said Watson. "Right on both points! But I confess that I don't see how you arrived at it. It was a sudden impulse upon my part, and I have mentioned it to no one."

Holmes traced back:

"Observation tells me that you have a little reddish mould adhering to your instep. Just opposite the Wigmore Street Office they have taken up the pavement and thrown up some earth, which lies in such a way that it is difficult to avoid treading in it in entering. The earth is of this peculiar reddish tint which is found, as far as I know, nowhere else in the neighbourhood. So much is observation. The rest is deduction."

"How, then, did you deduce the telegram?" asked Watson.

"Why, of course I knew that you had not written a letter, since I sat opposite [92] to you all morning. I see also in your open desk there that you have a sheet of stamps and a thick bundle of postcards. What could you go into the post-office for, then, but to send a wire? Eliminate all other factors, and the one which remains must be the truth."

"In this case it certainly is so," Watson replied after a little thought.

This intuition show shows that the process of backtracking involves not only reasoning, but also speculation.

见图略1

图略1 ：

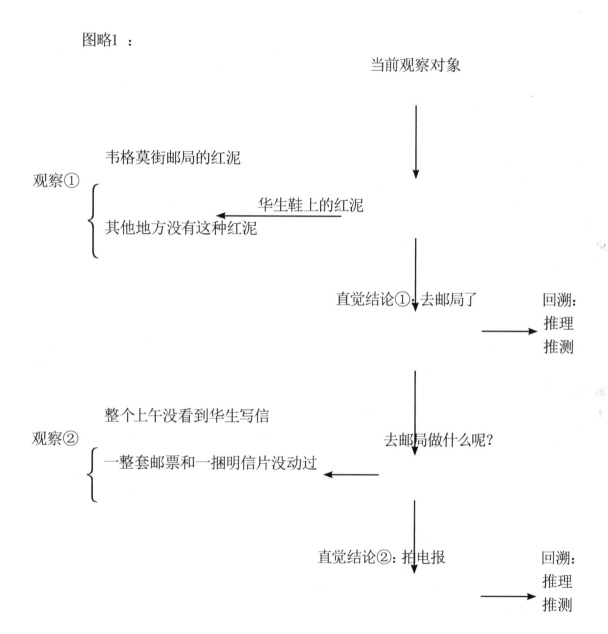

当前观察对象

观察① 韦格莫街邮局的红泥
其他地方没有这种红泥

华生鞋上的红泥

直觉结论①：去邮局了　　　回溯：推理 推测

观察② 整个上午没看到华生写信
一整套邮票和一捆明信片没动过

去邮局做什么呢？

直觉结论②：拍电报　　　回溯：推理 推测

见图略1See Sketch 1当前观察对象Current Observation 观察①ObjectObservation ①韦格莫街邮局的红泥The red mud of Wigmore Street Office其他地方没有这种红泥There is no such red mud in other places华生鞋上的红泥Red mud on Watson's 直觉结论①：去邮局了shoesIntuitive conclusion ①: You went to the post office回溯：推理 Backtracking: reasoning, deduction

C. Holmes' Intuition Show (No. 4):

Watson said,"I have heard you say it is difficult for a man to have any object in daily use without leaving the impress of his individuality upon it in such away that a trained observer might read it. Now, I have here a watch which has recently come into my possession. Would you have the kindness to let me have an opinion upon the character or habits of the late owner?"

Holmes said,"I should judge that the watch belonged to your elder brother, who inherited it from your father."

"That you gather, no doubt, from the H. W. upon the back?" asked Watson.

Holmes explained:

"Quite so. The W. suggests your own name. The date of the watch is nearly fifty years back, and the initials are as old as the watch: so it was made for the last generation. Jewellery usually descends to the eldest son, and he is most likely to have the same name as the father. Your father has, if I remember right, been dead many years. It has, therefore, been in the hands of your eldest brother."

"Right, so far," said Watson. "Anything else?"

"He was a man of untidy habits–very untidy and careless. He was left with good prospects, but he threw away his chances, lived for some time in poverty with occasional short intervals of prosperity, and finally, taking to drink, he died. That is all I can gather."

Watson sprang from my chair and limped impatiently about the room with considerable bitterness in my heart.

"This is unworthy of you, Holmes," Watson said. "I could not have believed that you would have descended to this. You have made inquiries into the history of my unhappy brother, and you now pretend to deduce this knowledge in some fanciful way. You cannot expect me to believe that you have read all this from his old watch! It is unkind and, to speak plainly, has a touch of charlatanism in it."

"My dear doctor," said Holmes kindly, "pray accept my apologies. Viewing the matter as an abstract problem, I had forgotten how personal and painful a thing it might be to you. I assure you, however, that I never even knew that you had a brother until you handed me the watch."

"Then how in the name of all that is wonderful did you get these facts?They are absolutely correct in every particular."

"When you observe the lower part of that watch-case you notice that it is not only dinted in two places but it is cut and marked all over from the habit of keeping other hard objects, such as coins or keys, in the same pocket. Surely it is no great feat to assume that a man who treats a fifty-guinea watch so cavalierly must be a careless man. Neither is it a very far-fetched inference that a man who inherits one article of such value is pretty well provided for in other respects."

"It is very customary for pawnbrokers in England, when they take a watch, to scratch the numbers of the ticket with a pin-point upon the inside of the case. It is more handy than a label as there is no risk of the number being lost or transposed. There are no less than four such numbers visible to my lens on the inside of this case. Inference–that your brother was often at low water. Secondary inference–that he had occasional bursts of prosperity, or he could not have redeemed the pledge. Finally, I ask you to look at the inner plate, which contains the keyhole.Look at the thousands of scratches all round the hole–marks where the key has slipped. What sober man's key could have scored those grooves?But you will never see a drunkard's watch without them. He winds it at night, and he leaves these traces of his unsteady hand. Where is the mystery in all this?" See Figure 2

图略2：

直觉结论 ——→回溯推理、推测

表 {
表盖：H ·W——→W 代表华生的姓；50年代的，刻字时间和制造时间相当；
上辈的遗产，贵重物品一般传长子
表底：邋遢粗心的人——→有创伤、损伤痕迹——→与硬币钥匙放一起
表侧：爱好酗酒——→上弦洞周围无数划痕——→上发条戳进钥匙所留——→酒后
双手发颤所致
表内：生活潦倒，偶尔很好——→当铺针刻四个号码，表明四次典当、赎回
}

See Sketch 2:

Intuitive Conclusion - → Retrospective Reasoning, Speculation

Table cover: H · W - → W represents the surname of Watson; In the 50s, the engraving time was comparable to the manufacturing time;

The legacy of the elders. Valuable items are generally passed on to the eldest son

Bottom of the table: Sloppy and careless people - → with signs of trauma and injury - → with coin keys

Table side: Hobbies for excessive drinking - → Numerous scratches around the upper chord hole - → Left by sticking the upper winding into the key - → Caused by trembling of both hands after drinking

Inside the table: Poor life, occasionally very good - → Pawnshop needle engraved with four numbers, indicating four times of pawning and redemption

D. Correctly understand Holmes' "guess".

When Holmes reasoned out that Watson had a poor brother who died of alcoholism through his pocket watch, he said to Holmes in surprise: "They are absolutely correct in every particular."

"Ah, that is good luck. I could only say what was the balance of probability. I did not at all expect to be so accurate."

"But it was not mere guesswork?"

"No, no: I never guess. It is a shocking habit–destructive to the logical faculty."

"The writer claimed by a momentary expression, a twitch of a muscle or a glance of an eye, to fathom a man's inmost thoughts."

"From a drop of water," said Holmes, "a logician could infer the possibility of an Atlantic or a Niagara without having seen or heard of one or the other."

When Watson asked about "florid face", Holmes said, "Ah, that was a more daring shot, though I have no doubt that I was right."

"The more I thought of it the more extraordinary did my companion's(referring to Holmes) hypothesis, that the man had been poisoned, appear."

"Through it, as you know, I came into possession of the pills, the existence of which I had already surmised."

"I've told you all I know myself now, for the rest is mere surmise and conjecture."

"...so I hazarded the opinion that the criminal was probably a robust and ruddy-faced man."

"There is nothing at all new to me in the latter part of your narrative except that you brought your own rope. That I did not know."

Especially Holmes said,"I should judge that the watch belonged to your elder brother, who inherited it from your father."

There are a lot of these words in this work.Is it not paradoxical that Holmes, while thinking and investigating with "guess", said "I never guess" and also said "It is a shocking habit"? In fact, we can "infer" according to the context. Holmes' "guess" here should be understood as guess without a basis, which is more in line with the original meaning.

2. The Statement of the Case

3. In Quenst of a Solution

4. The Story of the Bald-headed Man

5. The Tragedy of Pondicherry Lodge

6. Sherlock Holmes Gives a Demonstration

7. The Episode of the Barrel

8. The Baker Street Irregulars

9. A Break in the Chain

10. The End of the Islander

11. The Great Agra Treasure

12. The Strange Story of Jonathan

E. Holmes' investigative intuition:

The beautiful young Miss Mary Mostan's father was a senior captain officer stationed in India.When she was 17 years old, her father returned to England after visiting relatives. The telegram sent by his father from London said that he had arrived in London safely and stayed at the Langham Hotel.Her father urged her to get together as soon as possible. Once in London, she went straight to the Langham Hotel. Her father did live there, but he hasn't come back since he left the house the night before yesterday.She waited all day without news. At night, at the suggestion of the hotel manager, she reported the case and put a notice of looking for someone in the major newspapers the next day. From that day on, she had no news of her father.She often heard her father say that a major named Sholto was once a comrade in arms of a regiment. The major retired from the army some time ago and lived in Upper Norwood. Mostan contacted him, but he said he didn't even know his father was back in England. About six years ago, on May 4, 1882, the Times published an advertisement to find the address of Miss Mary Mostan. From the next day after she responded, she would receive an identical pearl of great value every year on the same day. But she couldn't find any clues about the sender. Miss Mostan then took out six pearls and a letter sent today, asking to meet her at 7:00 that evening and discuss something with her. It was a dilemma whether to go or not. For this matter, Miss Mostein came to Holmes for help.

After accepting the case, Holmes first went to consult the relevant materials, and came back to Watson with great enthusiasm, saying: "This case is not so mysterious, and these facts seem to have only one explanation."

"What? Have you found out the truth?" Watson asked eagerly.

"I can't say that yet. However, I found a suggestive fact, which is an extremely useful clue. Of course, some details need to be put together." This suggestive fact is that he found the obituary of Major Sholto's death on April 28, 1882 in the old Times. Watson could not see the effect of the obituary on the case."

Holmes, however, based on the existing materials and questions about the case, speculated:

Captain Mostan disappeared in London. He may only visit Major Sholto, but Sholto said that he did not know that Mostan had come to London. Four years later, Sholto died, and less than a week after his death, Miss Mostein received a valuable gift, which she would receive every year since. Now she received another letter, saying that she would be fair and that she was a wronged person. Apart from her father's death, what grievances did she have? What's more, only a few days after Sholto's death did gifts begin to be sent (dubious type)? Unless the descendants of Sholto knew the secret and wanted to make some compensation with these gifts (speculative type).—Holmes had a guess at this time that the case could not be separated from Major Sholto. This correct speculation has laid the right direction for investigation since then.

At seven o'clock in the evening, when Miss Mostan, Holmes and Watson made an appointment to meet the mysterious man, she brought a new information—drawings. The paper was made in India, and the drawing seemed to be a part of a building, with unreadable symbols, numbers and hieroglyphs written on it. Next to it, four people's signatures were written in crude handwriting: Jonathan Smore, Mohamed Singh, Abdullah Khan and Dest Akbar. Sherlock Holmes could not conclude that this had anything to do with the case! However, he was convinced that it was indeed an important document.

Holmes said, "Now I think the case is more profound and incomprehensible than I thought at first. I need to reorganize my thinking."—The case originally pointed to Major

Sholto, but now there were four more.Therefore, Holmes changed his mind according to the circumstances.

The mysterious person Miss Yomostein met was Thaddeus Sholto, the second son of Major Sholto.Holmes learned from him that his father had some secrets in his heart. He usually dares not go out alone, so he specially hires two boxers to guard the gate of Sakurama Villa.He never told the brothers what they were afraid of, but he was especially wary of people with wooden legs.Once, he injured a man with wooden legs with a gun.In the spring of 1882, Old Sholto received a letter from India. He almost fainted after reading the letter, and then fell ill. Until his death, neither of the brothers knew what the letter said.Old Sholto also disclosed the cause of Captain Mostan's death: they had experienced a series of strange events and gained a large fortune.He brought these treasures back to England.On the evening of Mostan's arrival in London, he came here to ask for his rightful share of the treasure.The two of them quarreled bitterly about how to divide the treasure equally.Mostan got up from his chair in a rage. Suddenly, he put his hand on his chest. His face was dark and he fell back. He hit the corner of the treasure chest and died.At the servant's suggestion, Mostan's body was buried that night. So old Sholto hoped to return the treasure of Mostan to Mostan's daughter—the fact confirmed Holmes' conjecture.

Just as Old Sholto was about to tell his brother where the two treasures were hidden, a figure outside the window scared him to death.The next morning, they found that the windows of their father's room were wide open, and the cabinets and boxes had been turned over but not stolen.Strangely, there was a piece of broken paper on his chest with "The Sign of Four" scribbled on it.They do not understand what these words mean, nor who the mysterious visitors are. But it can be concluded that this matter has something to do with his usual fear—— Another "The Sign of Four", Holmes was lost in thought.

Soon, the treasure worth 500000 pounds was found by the eldest son Bartholomeus in the sealed attic.The purpose of the Second Young Master, Miss Thaddeus Jomostein, is to ask for the treasures they deserve together.Holmes followed them to Pondicherry Lodges, the ancestral house where the eldest son lived, when the tragedy occurred.The eldest son died for several hours in a room with closed doors and windows.He sat on the chair, with a sad smile and a strange expression. His limbs were curled up, and his body was stiff and cold.Beside the table was a hammer like instrument with a stone tied with coarse twine. A piece of broken paper on the desk scrawled "The Sign of Four"—"The Sign of Four" again.

""It means murder," Holmes said confidently (conclusive type).

He then examined the body. ""Ah! I expected it. Look here!" (148) He pointed to a black thorn in the scalp above his ear -- a poisonous thorn——— This is what Holmes speculated.

"This is all an insoluble mystery to me," said Watson. "It grows darker instead of clearer."

"On the contrary," Holmes answered, "it clears every instant. I only require a few missing links to have an entirely connected case."

The second young Master found that the treasure box he helped to take out last night was robbed. Holmes asked him to go to the police and examined the case again. "My case is, as I have told you, almost complete; but we must not err on the side of overconfidence. Simple as the case seems now, there may be something deeper underlyingit."—At this time, Holmes reflected and tested the results of his previous speculation, indicating that he had a sophisticated dialectical thinking.

They continued to investigate the site and found that the windows were locked from the inside, the window frames were very solid, there were no hinges on either side, there were no rain pipes nearby, and the roof was very high.But there are boot marks on the windowsill, a thick boot with a wide iron palm on its heel, and a wooden pile mark.—This should be the man with wooden legs that Old Sholto feared. The wooden leg man appeared at the scene, adding new content to the investigation.

How did the criminal get in?The survey found that it should be from the entrance of the roof to the attic where the treasure was once hidden.Holmes and Watson went up the attic through the ladder and found that the floor was full of bare feet like children.Sherlock Holmes's face showed surprise."I was staggered for the moment," Holmes said, "but the thing is quite natural. My memory failed me, or I should have been able to foretell it."—What should Holmes have expected? In fact, it is a speculation about dwarfs. The work leaves a suspense here, which will be explained later.

In the face of the current situation, Watson was at a loss."It will be clear enough to you soon," Holmes said, in an offhand way. "I think that there is nothing else of importance here, but I will look."—Although Holmes knew it well, he still waited and waited to find more clues.

The expected clues appeared.It was found that a small footprint stepped on the strongly smelling creosote on the ground.So Holmes used Toby, a mixed breed dog that was very sensitive to smell, to track.After a series of ironic twists and turns, we finally arrived at the place we should go, the "Modikai Smith" boat rental company on the riverside.Through Mrs. Smith, we learned that the wooden leg man and the small man with monkey head and monkey brain had already rented the "Dawn" gas ship and left at three in the morning.Undoubtedly, they were the people who appeared at the scene of the crime. The next task was to track and catch the criminal.

Let's go back and say that when Sherlock Holmes found the creosote, Officer Jones and his party also arrived at the scene.After exchanging greetings with Holmes, he said to the case:The facts are clear here, and speculation is unnecessary.As far as I know, the door was locked, but the treasure worth 500000 pounds was lost.It is common sense that the footprints on the windowsill have nothing to do with the case when the window is closed firmly.Sholto confessed to staying with his brother last night. After his brother died in a rage, Sholto took the opportunity to take the jewels away.

"As you said, the dead man got up carefully and locked the door." Holmes said coldly.

Jones said there was a flaw.According to common sense, Thaddeus was with his brother and had a quarrel. Then his brother died and his jewels were lost. No one saw his brother since he left.Thaddeus is anxious and abnormal. He should be a suspect.— He only connected surface phenomena and labeled them as general "common sense".

"You haven't figured out all the facts yet," Holmes said. How can you explain the thorn and the scar?how can you explain this note and that stick inlaid with stone?

Jones said arrogantly that the room was full of Indian antiques.If this wood thorn was poisonous, Thaddeus could kill people with it just like anyone else.This piece of paper was just a trick.The only question is, how did he get out?He looked up and saw the hole in the roof, climbed up to check, and said that facts are better than theories.Now my idea has been fully confirmed: there is a secret door leading to the roof.Then he said to the second young Master, in view of your brother's death, he was arresting you on behalf of the government.

"I'm afraid the facts are not as simple as you think." Holmes said. He had to disclose the preliminary results of his investigation in advance:

There were two murderers who came to this room last night, one of whom I have reason to believe (conclusive type), his name is Jonathan Smaller (the first of "The Sign of Four").He is a middle-aged man with dark skin, low culture, short stature, and a flexible person. His right leg is amputated and equipped with a wooden leg, and the inner side of the wooden leg is rubbed off.There was a rough square forefoot on the sole of his left foot, and an iron palm was nailed to his heel. He was once a prisoner. Another one...

Holmes suddenly stopped, leaving Jones with a suspense.—The reader should know that he is the dwarf.This is also an account of the previous "I should have expected" speculation.Holmes learned from the "Geographic Dictionary" that the indigenous people of the Andaman Islands are the smallest people in the world, with deformed big heads, fierce small eyes, strange faces, and small hands and feet.The average height is less than four feet. They are vicious, irritable and stubborn by nature, but as long as we have established trust and friendship with them, they will not change until they die.They also often use wooden sticks with stones to smash the heads of the victims, or use poison arrows to shoot their opponents to death.—Holmes' extensive knowledge can be readily picked up in his work.

After that, with Holmes' careful planning and hard work, he found the hidden "Dawn" gas ship.Finally, with the cooperation of Jones and other police officers, they carried out a soul stirring and dangerous hunt for the people involved in the case on the "Dawn" gas ship, and finally shot the dwarfs into the water and arrested Smaller.

THE ADVENTURES OF SHERLOCK HOLMES

1. A Scandal in Bohemia

A. Holmes' Intuition Show (No. 5):

HOLMES SAID TO WATSON:"AND IN PRACTICE AGAIN, I OBSERVE. YOU DID NOT TELL ME THAT you intended to go into harness."

"Then, how do you know?" asked Watson.

Holmes reasoned:

"As to your practice, if a gentleman walks into my rooms smelling of iodoform, with a black mark of nitrate of silver upon his right forefinger, and a bulge on the right side of his top-hat to show where he has secreted his stethoscope, I must be dull, indeed, if I do not pronounce him to be an active member of the medical profession."

B. Holmes' Intuition Show (No. 6):

Holmes saw that the Watson family "have a most clumsy and careless servant girl."

Watson said: She is incorrigible, and my wife has given her notice. "But there, again, I fail to see how you work it out."

Holmes backtracked:

"...my eyes tell me that on the inside of your left shoe, just where the firelight strikes it, the leather is scored by six almost parallel cuts. Obviously they have been caused by someone who has very carelessly scraped round the edges of the sole in order to remove crusted mud from it. Hence, you see, my double deduction that you had been out in vile weather, and that you had a particularly malignant boot-slitting specimen of the London slavey."

C. Holmes' difference between "seeing" and "observing":

Seeing, the main definitions of modern Chinese are as follows: First, make your eyes contact people or things; Second, observe and judge. Observation, the main definition of modern Chinese is to carefully look at things or phenomena.Although the former also has the meaning of the latter, Holmes believes that there is a big difference between "seeing" and "observing". Holmes gave Watson an example to illustrate:

"...you have frequently seen the steps which lead up from the hall to this room."

Watson:"Frequently."

Holmes:"How often?"

Watson:"Well, some hundreds of times."

Holmes:"Then how many are there?"

Watson:"How many? I don't know."

"Quite so! You have not observed. And yet you have seen. That is just my point. Now, I know that there are seventeen steps, because I have both seen and observed." Holmes' meaning can be understood as that "seeing" belongs to the state of blindness, which is a state of direct perception without the participation of thinking; observation belongs to the level of concentration, and participation of thinking, which is far from each other. It can be seen that Holmes' thinking is rigorous and meticulous.

2. The Red-headed League

Wilson, the owner of a small pawnshop with red hair, seems to have taken his luck recently.Spolding, the only clerk in the shop, told him that red hair would advertise and recruit red hair men as part-time workers, so they could work easily and earn super high salaries.At the instigation of his partner, Wilson applied for the job.Although the applicants are crowded and the conditions are harsh, the recruiter Duncan seems to particularly like Wilson—he was admitted!The job content is to copy the "Encyclopedia Britannica" in the office of the company for four hours every day with ink and paper. You are not allowed to leave the company for any reason, or you will be fired.The business of the small pawnshop is poor, so he naturally cherishes this part-time job.Wilson was also touched by the enthusiastic waiter who said that he would take the initiative to undertake the work in the store during his part-time job.One day eight weeks later, when he arrived at the company on time, he found that the iron general of the office was guarding the door, with a card on the door, on which was written the revelation of the dissolution of the Red Hair Association.Wilson, confused, became Holmes's guest.

MASTER OF INTUITION: SHERLOCK HOLMES

A. Holmes' Intuition Show (No. 7):

Wilson came to the Baker Street apartment. After they had a look, Holmes said to Watson.

"Beyond the obvious facts that he has at some time done manual labour, that he takes snuff, that he is a Freemason, that he has been in China, and that he has done a considerable amount of writing lately, I can deduce nothing else."

"How, in the name of good-fortune, did you know all that, Mr. Holmes?" Mr. Wilson suddenly raised his head and asked. "How did you know, for example, that I did manual labour? It's as true as gospel, for I began as a ship's carpenter."

Holmes reasoned:

"Your hands, my dear sir. Your right hand is quite a size larger than your left. You have worked with it, and the muscles are more developed."

"Well, the snuff, then, and the Freemasonry?"

"I won't insult your intelligence by telling you how I read that, especially as, rather against the strict rules of your order, you use an arc-and-compass breastpin."

"Ah, of course, I forgot that. But the writing?"

"What else can be indicated by that right cuff so very shiny for five inches, and the left one with the smooth patch near the elbow where you rest it upon the desk?"

"Well, but China?"

"The fish that you have tattooed immediately above your right wrist could only have been done in China. I have made a small study of tattoo marks and have even contributed to the literature of the subject. That trick of staining the fishes' scales of a delicate pink is quite peculiar to China.When, in addition, I see a Chinese coin hanging from your watch-chain, the matter becomes even more simple." Mr. Jabez Wilson laughed heavily. "Well, I never!" said he. "I thought at first that you had done something clever, but I see that there was nothing in it, after all."

Intuitive conclusions often burst into people's minds, leaving them unprepared and thinking that they were the great immortals who had predicted everything; retrospective reasoning peels off the cocoon, advances step by step, and unveils the mystery. So it is!

B. Understanding of Watson's relationship between "reasoning" and "intuition":

"I knew well, he was never so truly formidable as when, for days on end, he had been lounging in his armchair amid his improvisations and his black-letter editions. Then it was that the lust of the chase would suddenly come upon him, and that his brilliant reasoning power would rise to the level of intuition, until those who were unacquainted with his methods would look askance at him as on a man whose knowledge was not that of other mortals."

Reasoning and intuition have different responsibilities. If intuition charges ahead, then reasoning is behind the palace. There is no higher and lower, let alone the problem that intuition is higher than reasoning; In terms of meaning, the former is also better understood, while the latter is obscure. In fact, what the author really wants to express is that "the reasoning process is condensed into intuition". Because intuition is also called concentrated thinking, or thinking that goes beyond the reasoning process to the results.

In fact, Watson's "a man whose knowledge was not that of other mortals" behavior should refer to the "divine operation" brought about by intuition. This shows that Watson is very familiar with intuition. Indeed, "divine operation" is the externalization and crystallization of intuitive thinking. For example, Holmes' series of intuition shows are typical "divine operation". There are numerous cases of "divine operation" in the investigation, which will not be repeated here.

C. Analysis of Watson's doubts:

Watson said: "I trust that I am not more dense than my neighbours, but I was always oppressed with a sense of my own stupidity in my dealings with Sherlock Holmes. Here I had heard what he had heard, I had seen what he had seen, and yet from his words it was evident that he saw clearly not only what had happened but what was about to happen, while to me the whole business was still confused and grotesque. As I drove home to my house in Kensington I thought over it all, from the extraordinary story of the red-headed copier of the Encyclopaedia down to the visit to Saxe-Coburg Square, and the ominous words with which he had parted from me. What was this nocturnal expedition, and why should I go armed? Where were we going, and what were we to do? I had the hint from Holmes that this smooth-faced pawnbroker's assistant was a formidable man—a man who might play a deep game. I tried to puzzle it out, but gave it up in despair and set the matter aside until night should bring an explanation."

This is caused by the gap between observation and intuition.

Although Holmes was a "co policeman" or a private detective, to be exact, he loved the investigation work almost to the point of neglecting sleep and food, being crazy and not afraid of sacrifice. In a word, these aspects are worth learning:

First, we should have the lofty spirit of dedication, rigorous working attitude, and a high degree of love for the profession;

Second, we should attach great importance to the cultivation and sharpening of observation, because observation is the only way to intuitive thinking. Otherwise, although "I heard everything he heard and I saw everything he saw", "I" cannot see the essence through the phenomenon, let alone the internal law of the development of things;

Third, we should increase the scope of knowledge, multi-disciplinary and multi-level knowledge reserves, which can make intuitive thinking come from both sides and understand by analogy;

Fourth, we should improve professional depth. Deep professional knowledge can reduce and avoid the deviation and inaccuracy of intuitive thinking, and effectively improve the accuracy of intuitive thinking.

D. Holmes' Intuitive Investigation:

1. There will be a major case in Saxe-Coburg Square tonight.

Perhaps the relaxed concert brought Holmes an epiphany. When he and Watson heard the music, he said to Watson: There would be a major case in Saxe-Coburg Square(conclusive). And because it was Saturday, time became urgent. He and Watson should meet in Baker Street at ten o'clock in the evening, and Watson should take his pistol with him.

"And how could you tell that they would make their attempt to-night?" Watson asked.

Holmes explained:

When they closed their League offices that was a sign that they cared no longer about Mr. Jabez Wilson's presence—in other words, that they had completed their tunnel. But it was essential that they should use it soon, as it might be discovered, or the bullion might be removed.Saturday would suit them better than any other day, as it would give them two days for their escape. For all these reasons I expected them to come to-night.

It turned out so.

2. Speculation on the special motives of a pawnshop assistant.

Holmes said: From the time I heard that the guy was only getting half his salary, I could see that he obviously had some special motive. I didn't know what the motive was.

"How did you guess his motives?" Watson asked.

Holmes guessed and reasoned that their purpose was banking step by step according to his series of questions:

Had there been women in the house, I should have suspected a mere vulgar intrigue. That, however, was out of the question. The man's business was a small one, and there was nothing in his house which could account for such elaborate preparations, and such an expenditure as they were at. It must, then, be something out of the house. What could it be?(Doubt 1) I thought of the assistant's fondness for photography, and his trick of vanishing into the cellar. The cellar! There was the end of this tangled clue. Then I made inquiries as to this mysterious assistant and found that I had to deal with one of the coolest and most daring criminals in London.He was doing something in the cellar– something which took many hours a day for months on end. What could it be, once more?(Doubt 2) I could think of (Speculation type)7nothing save that he was running a tunnel to some other building.

So far I had got when we went to visit the scene of action. I surprised you by beating upon the pavement with my stick. I was ascertaining whether the cellar stretched out in front or behind. It was not in front.Then I rang the bell, and, as I hoped, the assistant answered it. We have had some skirmishes, but we had never set eyes upon each other before. I hardly looked at his face. His knees were what I wished to see. You must yourself have remarked how worn, wrinkled, and stained they were. They spoke of those hours of burrowing. The only remaining point was what they were burrowing for. (Doubt 3) I walked round the corner, saw the City and Suburban Bank abutted on our friend's premises, and felt that I had solved my problem(Conclusion after the clarification).

In fact, Holmes' doubts are far more than these. Here is a list of relevant contents found in the works as much as possible, expressed by simple and clear diagrams. See Figure 3.

图略3:

Sketch 3:

作品中发现的相关疑点（存疑型—多疑式）：

Relevant doubts found in the work (doubt type):

1. 广告有点不合常规；

1.This advertisement is a bit unconventional;

2. 伙计自愿拿一半工资；

2.The assistant volunteered to take half of his salary;

3. 广告和伙计一样非同寻常；

3.This advertisement is as unusual as this assistant;

4. 伙计喜欢拍照并常常在地下室冲洗；

4. The assistant likes to take photos and often washes in the cellar;

5. 伙计拿着广告主动找威尔逊；

5. The assistant took the advertisement actively to find Wilson;

6. 伙计似乎对这事很了解；

6. The assistant seems to know this very well;

7. 我"看到应聘者太多准备放弃时，伙计不赞成；

7.When "I" saw too many candidates ready to give up, the assistant disagreed;

8. 招聘者邓肯对 "我" 兴趣浓厚, 关门谈话;

8.The recruiter Duncan was very interested in "me" and closed the door to talk with "me";

9. "我" 怕耽误典当行的生意, 伙计说: "不碍事, 我会替你照看";

9. "I" was afraid of delaying the pawnshop's business. The assistant said, "It's OK, I'll take care of it for you";

10. 所谓工作就是在办公室抄写《大英百科全书》, 不许离开;

10. The so-called job was to copy the Encyclopaedia in the office and not to leave;

11. 每天4个小时, 丰厚而简单的 "工作" 令人难以置信;

11.Four hours a day, the simple "work" with rich income was unbelievable;

12.8个星期后红发会解散, "邓肯" 失踪;

12.Eight weeks later, the Red Hair Association was dissolved, and "Duncan" disappeared;

13. 伙计安慰我等等看, 也许会收到来信。

13.The assistant comforted me to wait and see. Maybe I would get a letter.

It can be seen from the above cases that conclusion, doubt, speculation and insight are all forms of intuitive thinking, but their production methods are very different.The appearance of insight is a sudden sensation unexpected, such as lightning across the sky, and a flash of light, like a ghost coming and going without a trace; The latter three are active fighters, who aim at the current problems, situations or individual operations, or carry on the past and follow the future. They can be divided and combined freely, coexist harmoniously, and fight together until the owner is satisfied.

When the confident conclusion type suddenly finds a new information, the thinking will immediately turn to the skeptical type, seeking breakthrough, or may jump to the "foresight" type of speculation.Those who firmly believe in the results of speculation return to the conclusion type, and those who have uncertain results return to the suspect type. This is repeated until the result of ideal thinking is achieved.

3. A Case of Identity

A. Holmes' Intuition Show (No. 8):

successfully created the image of Sherlock Holmes and attracted the readers. In these intuition shows, we not only saw Holmes' sharp, rapid and accurate intuitive thinking, but also saw Holmes' meticulous and rigorous logical reasoning ability.meticulous and rigorous logical reasoning ability.

When Miss Mary Sutherland came to visit, Holmes asked her to sit down in the armchair, and for a moment looked at her with his characteristic absent mindedness. Then he said:

"Do you not find," he said, "that with your short sight it is a little trying to do so much typewriting?"

"I did at first," she answered, "but now I know where the letters are without looking." Then, suddenly realizing the full purport of his words, she gave a violent start and looked up, with fear and astonishment upon her broad, good-humoured face. "You've heard about me, Mr. Holmes," she cried, "else how could you know all that?"

"Never mind," said Holmes, laughing; "it is my business to know things. Perhaps I have trained myself to see what others overlook. If not, why should you come to consult me?"

How did Holmes know Miss Mary Sutherland's myopia and career? Later, he explained to Watson:

"I then glanced at her face, and, observing the dint of a pince-nez at either side of her nose, I ventured a remark upon short sight and typewriting, which seemed to surprise her." These are actually two conjectures that Holmes boldly put forward.

B. The observation difference between Watson and Holmes:

As for the observation of Miss Mary Sutherland, see what is the difference between Watson and Holmes.

Holmes said to Watson, "Now, what did you gatNow, what did you gather from that woman's appearance? Describe it."

Watson said:"Well, she had a slate-coloured, broad-brimmed straw hat, with a feather of a brickish red. Her jacket was black, with black beads sewn upon it, and a fringe of little black jet ornaments. Her dress was brown, rather darker than coffee colour, with a little purple plush at the neck and sleeves. Her gloves were grayish and were worn through at the right forefinger. Her boots I didn't observe. She had small round, hanging gold earrings, and a general air of being fairly well-to-do in a vulgar, comfortable, easy-going way."

Sherlock Holmes clapped his hands softly together and chuckled:"Pon my word, Watson, you are coming along wonderfully. You have really done very well indeed. It is true that you have missed everything of importance, but you have hit upon the method, and you have a quick eye for colour. Never trust to general impressions, my boy, but concentrate yourself upon details. My first glance is always at a woman's sleeve. In a man it is perhaps better first to take the knee of the trouser. As you observe, this woman had plush upon her sleeves, which is a most useful material for showing traces. The double line a little above the wrist, where the typewritist presses against the table, was beautifully defined.The sewing-machine, of the hand type, leaves a similar mark, but only on the left arm, and on the side of it farthest from the thumb, instead of being right across the broadest part, as this was. I then glanced at her face, and, observing the dint of a pince-nez at either side of her nose, I ventured a remark upon short sight and typewriting, which seemed to surprise her."

"I was then much surprised and interested on glancing down to observe that, though the boots which she was wearing were not unlike each other, they were really odd ones; the one having a slightly decorated toe-cap, and the other a plain one. One was buttoned only in the two lower buttons out of five, and the other at the first, third, and fifth. Now, when you see that a young lady, otherwise neatly dressed, has come away from home with odd boots, half-buttoned, it is no great deduction to say that she came away in a hurry."

From their observation of Miss Mary Sutherland, Watson's observation, from appearance to appearance, has no focus and lacks directivity; Holmes' observations are quite different, ranging from broad to detailed, focusing on the key points, especially on different genders, which is worth learning.

4. The Boscombe Valley Mystery

Analysis of Watson's "Doctor's Intuition":

Watson asked: "Might not the nature of the injuries reveal something to my medical instincts?"

Is there a relationship between career and intuition?

The answer is yes. Profession is closely related to intuition. From the horizontal perspective, professions dealing with people and things are conducive to the development of intuitive thinking;professions dealing with words and figures are conducive to the growth of logical thinking. From the vertical point of view, the intuitive thinking of different occupations has considerable career orientation or tendentiousness. A netizen said: A policeman look at your eyes and knows if you are a criminal; a traffic policeman looks at your face and knows if you have drunk;a doctor looks at your face and knows if you are ill.In a teacher's opinion, whether the students can pass the exam will be determined by their usual scores.In the TV drama "Detective Tang Lang, "the thief said more frankly: "Brother Lang has a police instinct, but I have a thief's instinct!"

5. The Five Orange Pips

A. Holmes' Intuition Show (No. 9):

As soon as the client entered the room, Holmes said to him politely: "You have come up from the south-west, I see."

The client said:"Yes, from Horsham."

Then Holmes explained:"That clay and chalk mixture which I see upon your toe caps is quite distinctive."

B. Holmes' guess of inaccuracy:

One autumn equinox night, the wind was howling and the rain was pouring. The doorbell in Baker Street rang suddenly.

"Why," said Watson, glancing up at Holmes, "that was surely the bell.Who could come to-night? Some friend of yours, perhaps?"

"Except yourself I have none," he answered. "I do not encourage visitors."

"A client, then?"

"If so, it is a serious case. Nothing less would bring a man out on such a day and at such an hour. But I take it that it is more likely to be some crony of the landlady's."

Holmes guessed wrong, because footsteps sounded in the corridor, and then someone knocked at the door. The visitor was indeed the client.

Of course, Holmes is not an immortal, not an ever victorious general, and cannot win every battle. In Sherlock Holmes' words,"I have been beaten four times—three times by men, and once by a woman."

C. Holmes' understanding of "intuition" in this work:

In the work, Holmes said a lot about reasoning and intuition to Watson when he was thinking about the investigation plan. On intuition, he said: "Problems may be solved in the study which have baffled all those who have sought a solution by the aid of their senses."

Although intuition has powerful functions and outstanding achievements, it cannot be invincible and dominate the world. It is definitely not possible and impossible to rely solely on intuition. This is consistent with Holmes' consistent view of intuition.

In "A Study in Scarlet," Holmes introduced himself as follows:"Well, I have a trade of my own. I suppose I am the only one in the world. I'm a consulting detective, if you can understand what that is. Here in London we have lots of government detectives and lots of private ones.When these fellows are at fault, they come to me, and I manage to put them on the right scent. They lay all the evidence before me, and I am generally able, by the help of my knowledge of the history of crime, to set them straight."

"But do you mean to say," Watson said, "that without leaving your room you can unravel some knot which other men can make nothing of, although they have seen every detail for themselves?"

Holmes said:"Quite so. I have a kind of intuition that way."

What Holmes meant was that many detectives inside and outside the system would come to him for consultation when they encountered problems or cases that could not be solved. As long as they provided relevant clues, evidence and facts, he could solve it without leaving home. And his time tested "weapon" was his proud intuitive thinking!

This is not only Holmes' full affirmation of the powerful ability of intuition, but also a highly self praise of his ability and level to solve problems with intuition.

Of course, Holmes went on to say, "Now and again a case turns up which is a little more complex. Then I have to bustle about and see things with my own eyes." That is to say, simple cases can be solved by his intuition, and only slightly complicated cases can he investigate in person.

The work also describes the important guiding role of intuition in case investigation for Holmes when he was at a loss.

The Bruce-Parttington Plans: "Our scent runs cold here... My instinct now is to work from the other end." Holmes' intuition points out the right direction for him in the case investigation.

"The Disappearance of Lady Frances Carfax":Lady Frances Carfax has been missing for many days. Holmes and Watson have searched for many places without success. When they were at a loss, Holmes said: "All my instincts tell me that she is in London, but as we have at present [948] no possible means of telling where...My intuition tells me that she is in London, but we cannot tell where she is at present..." Lady Frances Carfax is indeed in London, and she has been controlled by Shlessinger.

The work also describes the perspective function of Holmes' intuition on people and things.

"The Creeping Man":"...and I have the greatest confidence in her intuition..." This is Holmes's comment on the professor's daughter Edith after a one-sided acquaintance.

"The Lion's Mane": Holmes said, ""I value a woman's instinct in such matters. You use the word 'they.' You think that more than one was concerned?" This "in some matters" refers to interpersonal relations. This is Holmes' full affirmation of women's relatively accurate intuition in this regard.

These Holmes' intuitions fully illustrate from different aspects that intuition is his eyes, his thinking, and his "weapon". Intuition is indispensable in his daily life, especially in the investigation work, and its contribution cannot be denied!

6. The Man with the Twisted Lip(not involved)

7. The Adventure of the Blue Carbuncle

A. Holmes' Intuition Show (No. 10):

In Chinese, "pie in the sky" means to enjoy something without contributing. Peterson, the doorman, had such a good thing last night. He picked up a big fat goose and a broken felt hat. He took these two things to Holmes' house to show him who their owners were. Although the goose leg was tied with a small card that said "To Mrs. Henry Baker"; Holmes also felt powerless because of the initials "H.B." in the worn felt hat. Peterson had to take the goose away and leave the broken felt hat to Holmes to study.

Just as Watson came to visit, Holmes said to Watson, "What can you gather yourself as to the individuality of the man who has worn this article?"

Watson took the tattered object in my hands and turned it over rather ruefully.It was a very ordinary black hat of the usual round shape, hard and much the worse for wear. The lining had been of red silk, but was a good deal discoloured. There was no maker's name; but, as Holmes had remarked, the initials "H. B." were scrawled upon one side. It was pierced in the brim for a hat-securer, but the elastic was missing. For the rest, it was cracked, exceedingly dusty, and spotted in several places, although there seemed to have been some attempt to hide the discoloured patches by smearing them with ink.

Watson said he couldn't see anything. Then Holmes began to "show" his intuition and reasoning:

The owner of the hat was a knowledgeable person: although Holmes did not mention it in his reasoning, his appearance was indeed the same when he met, which showed that Holmes was accurate in his speculation. He was a large man with rounded shoulders, a massive head.He spoke in a slow staccato fashion, choosing his words with care, and gave the impression generally of a man of learning and letters who had had ill-usage at the hands of fortune.

Family affairs are in decline: this hat has been bought for three years. This kind of hat with flat brim and rolled up brim was very fashionable at that time. The hat is of good quality, which can be felt from the threaded silk straps and the luxurious lining. If he bought this expensive hat three years ago and hasn't bought a hat since, it means that he is getting worse every year.

There is "foresight", but also "decadent": this is his customized hat. From the small round buttons and straps used to fasten elastic belts, we can see that this man has foresight, and the hats sold never carry these things. This is to prevent the hat from being blown away. We also saw that he had broken the elastic band and was unwilling to put another one on. This shows that his will is getting more and more depressed.

Dust on hat: It is the dark brown flocculent dust in the room. It means the hat is hung in the room most of the time.

Sweat stains on the lining: It indicates that the person wearing the hat often sweats a lot and is a weak person.

The relationship between husband and wife is not harmonious: maybe he is affected by some bad behavior, maybe he has the bad habit of drinking, which is also the reason why his wife no longer loves him.

He didn't have a gas lamp in his house: there were one or two drops of wax tears on his hat, which might have been accidentally dropped, but I saw at least five drops of wax tears on his hat. There was no doubt that the wax tears must have been dropped because of frequent contact with the burning candle.

In addition, there are results directly obtained after observation:

Middle aged, gray hair, just had a haircut and applied lemon cream: there are many hair haws on the lining, and the smell of lemon cream.

He is not a bachelor: the card on the goose leg shows that he is taking the goose home as a goodwill gift to his wife.

Multi angle and multi-level speculation on human personality is psychological portrait. It can be seen from this that Sherlock Holmes is probably the originator of the psychological portrait!

B. The understanding of "conjecture" and "surmise" in the works.

When Mr. Baker, the owner of the broken felt hat, appeared in Holmes' apartment on Baker Street, the work described as follows: These characteristics remind people of Holmes' surmise about him.

Conjecture is defined as speculation based on imagination without objective evidence. From the above interpretation, it can be concluded that "conjecture" is basically a purely subjective thing, not a speculation based on objective facts and evidence. In other words, "conjecture" is "blind speculation".

However, Holmes' psychological portrait of the hat owner in the work—intuitive speculation is obviously very accurate. Why is it still called "conjecture"? This is obviously contrary to the original meaning of the original text and the original meaning of the hero.

Speculation is to infer the unknown on the basis of the known, which is the product of the facts.

In addition, there is a sentence in the Study of Blood Characters: "I've told you all I know myself now, for the rest is mere surmise and conjecture."

"Guess" is a guess made based on certain clues; "Assumption" is a decision made based on "blind guess". Although the meanings of the two are not diametrically opposed, they are also far apart. Therefore, the juxtaposition of "guess and assumption" does not hold.

8. The Speckled Band

A. The understanding of "the rapid deductions, as swift as intuitions":

"I had no keener pleasure than in following Holmes in his professional investigations, and in admiring the rapid deductions, as swift as intuitions, and yet always founded on a logical basis, with which he unravelled the problems which were submitted to him."

This sentence should at least contain the following meanings:

First, Holmes' intuition is very sharp and fast;

Second, Holmes' intuition is very accurate, which is basically verified by logic;

Third, Holmes solved many "difficult and miscellaneous problems" of his clients by his quick and accurate intuitive thinking.

B. Holmes' Intuition Show (No. 11):

After the client, Miss Helen Stoner, entered the Baker Street apartment, Holmes quickly looked her up and down.

Folmes said:"You have come in by train this morning, I see." "You must have started early, and yet you had a good drive in a dog-cart, along heavy roads, before you reached the station."

"You know me, then?" Miss Helen Stoner said, gazing at Holmes in bewilderment.

Holmes explained:

"No, but I observe the second half of a return ticket in the palm of your left glove. You must have started early, and yet you had a good drive in a dog-cart, along heavy roads, before you reached the station."

"Whatever your reasons may be, you are perfectly correct," said she. "I started from home before six, reached Leatherhead at twenty past, and came in by the first train to Waterloo.

C. Suspicions in Sherlock Holmes' Investigation:

1. "My attention was speedily drawn, as I have already remarked to you, to this ventilator, and to the bell-rope which hung down to the bed."

     Explanation: "The discovery that this was a dummy, and that the bed was clamped to the floor, instantly gave rise to the suspicion that the rope was there as a bridge for something passing through the hole and coming to the bed.The idea of a snake instantly occurred to me..."

2. Holmes had doubts after checking the bedroom of Miss Helen Stoner and the doctor:

     However, "The sight of the safe, the saucer of milk, and the loop of whipcord were enough to finally dispel any doubts which may have remained." Holmes said.

     Explanation: The doubt is that Holmes still can't figure out the real cause of the death of Miss Helen Stoner's sister; it turns out that the safe is the place to store poisonous snakes, milk is the food of poisonous snakes, and the knots of whip ropes are used to trap poisonous snakes.

9. The Engineer's Thumb

Observation of the victim and the perpetrator—intuition field (incorporated into "The Final Problem")

10. The Noble Bachelor

A. Holmes' "Conclusion".

The Lord St.Simon had a strange unfortunate event when he was holding his wedding, which made the city full of wind and rain, and many newspapers rushed to report it. After reading these newspapers, Holmes seemed to have a clear idea of the mysterious bride disappearance—there was an intuitive judgment.He said to Watson: "I had formed my conclusions as to the case before our client came into the room." This "conclusion" is very consistent with the form and content of conclusion intuition. So, what is the conclusion? It's the bride who lost herself! Of course, it is impossible to tell the reader at the beginning of the work, otherwise the reader will not have suspense. When Holmes received the client, Lord Robert St. Simon, he learned the following information with a clear aim around his conclusion:

First, Robert and Miss Dolan met one year ago when they were traveling in the United States;

Second, although they have no engagement, they maintain friendly exchanges;

Third, when she came with her father to participate in social activities at the end of the year in London, he contacted her many times and signed an engagement until marriage;

Fourth, Miss Dolan was in a happy mood before and after the wedding;

Fifthly, Robert thought there was a trivial detail that caught Holmes' attention: when they walked to the vestry of the church, the flowers in her hands fell on the floor of the front row seats, and a gentleman in the seats picked them up and handed them to her. After that, she was uneasy;

Sixth, after returning to Doran's father's apartment, when she and her American maid Alice whispered, Robert heard something like "forcibly occupying other people's land";

Seventh, after sitting for about ten minutes at breakfast, she got up and said a few words of apology before leaving the room. Alice, the maid, said that Doran went into her room, took a long coat and put it on the bride's dress, put on a soft hat and went out;

Eighth, someone saw her walk into Hyde Park with Robert's ex girlfriend Miller. Robert said the police thought his ex girlfriend had killed Dolan;

Ninth, they could see the park across from the breakfast table.

Through the above inquiry, Holmes was more confident—no doubt confirmed his conclusion. He said to Robert:I've settled... I mean, I've settled the case... I'll be able to provide details soon.What This made Robert completely confused.

In addition, Holmes saw the bill of the luxury hotel and the note with the initials from the visiting police officer Lestrade, and revealed his conclusion to Lestrade: "Lady St. Simon is a myth. There is not, and there never has been, any such person."

Without the long-term accumulation of relevant knowledge, Holmes could not have foreseen the case with great confidence."I have notes of several similar cases, though none, as I remarked before, which were quite as prompt. My whole examination served to turn my conjecture into a certainty." "There was a parallel instance in Aberdeen some years back, and something on very much the same lines at Munich the year after the Franco-Prussian War."

B. Lestrade's Inaccurate Intuition:

On the contrary to Sherlock Holmes, Officer Lestrade had no idea about the case of Lord St.Simon's marriage.

When he heard that the bride and Robert's ex girlfriend Millar walked into Hyde Park, he thought that the bride's disappearance was related to her;

When he found a note in the bride's dress discarded by the lake, he thought that Miller had set a trap to lure the bride away (in fact, it was written by the bride's ex husband Frank), and confidently believed that since the dress was there, the body would not be too far away, so he fished for the "body" in the lake.

When Holmes teased Lestrade about his "professionalism", he also retorted:"I believe in hard work and not in sitting by the fire spinning fine theories." Lestrade clearly meant that Holmes was an empty theorist who only knew what he was talking about on paper and talked about "observation—reasoning" in vain. He is a down-to-earth, pragmatic doer.He pretends to be a policeman within the system, which is not imminent. He neither introspects himself and checks whether he investigates the case in depth, nor grasps all kinds of background information before the crime, so that his intuition is inaccurate;he is hasty, and he is beaten by the facts.

11. The Beryl Coronet

Understanding of Watson's intuition about women:

When Watson talked about the love process between him and Miss Morstan in "The Sign of Four," he sweetly recalled:"...as she has often told me, there was in her also the instinct to turn to me for comfort and protection. So we stood hand in hand like two children, and there was peace in our hearts for all the dark things that surrounded us."

What did Miss Morstan intuitively know about Watson? Although there is no specific description, it can be seen from Watson's words and deeds that he is mature and stable, does not admire vanity, is honest, responsible, and dare to take responsibility. Therefore, Miss Morstan's intuition believed that Watson was a good man who was worthy of being entrusted for life.

In "The Boscombe Valley Mystery," there was a similar description of Miss Turner:"... with a woman's quick intuition, fastening upon my companion..."

Mary in this work "...has a woman's quick insight into character." Although the word "intuition" is not used here, we have previously introduced that insight is the core of intuition, and insight can be understood as intuition here. As a woman, Mary has the ability of intuitive personality.

This leads to the question, is a woman's intuition particularly sensitive and accurate?

Before answering this question, we should first talk about whether gender is related to the strength of intuition. It should be said that gender has no inevitable relationship with the strength of intuition, that is, it is difficult for men and women to say which is stronger and which is weaker. We often hear that women's intuition is particularly accurate. After a little analysis, we will find that women's intuition is really unusual in people's daily life. To be specific, women's intuition in interpersonal relationships and business relationships is extraordinary, and they are often better than men. An example in the book "Top Secret Operation of Mossad in Israel" illustrates the problem:

Samira, the wife of Halim (an Iraqi nuclear scientist), finally returned to Paris from Iraq (her husband studied in a nuclear factory in France). She found that her husband had changed a lot these days when she left. She became more generous and smart, and her clothes were more neat and exquisite, which was a bit strange. Halim explained that he had raised his salary again and now he was rich. Seeing that Samira was suspicious of his words, Halim told his wife about what happened these days (a German businessman wanted to buy nuclear reactor information, and he and his friends said he was a CIA agent). Samira said to him immediately: "Do you think those German businessmen are really CIA people?"

"Donovan said it was the CIA," said Halim

Samira became angry, and she said loudly: "You don't think about it. Why does the CIA want to know about these? Those people must be Israeli intelligence personnel."

Halim was shocked. He said, "How do you know they are Israelis?"

Samira said, "I follow a woman's intuition. Who is willing to ask for trouble with you except the Israelis and my silly woman?"

Women's intuition is sometimes accurate. Samira did not guess wrong.

Samira, Halim's wife, can be said to have sharp eyes. She is not an anti espionage officer, but she is a woman, a wife, and a sensitive region in sectarian strife —the Middle East. These are the basis and background of Samira's keen intuition. However, what triggered her intuition was that some minor changes in her husband's daily life and interpersonal communication made her suspicious, and she speculated that her husband had made significant changes in his work career. What exactly was it? She didn't know. The lies made up by her husband did not let the wife know. When her husband told the whole story of his business with a German businessman to buy nuclear reactor materials, based on her understanding of her husband and his sensitive work, she deduced the terrible fact that her husband had been targeted by Israeli spies. Although Halim's wife "saw through" a spy case, it does not show her talent in counterespionage, but only the

54

excellent intuitive performance of women in interpersonal relationships. As for whether the intuition of women in other fields and industries is higher than that of men, there is no research.

It is worth mentioning that the book also draws an equal sign between "intuition" and "guess".

12. The Copper Beeches

Timely and Accurate Information Is the Basis for Correct Speculation:

Miss Hunter, a governess who lived in a dilemma and was almost penniless, was taken care of by Lucas, a generous and amiable client at the employment agency. The job was easy, the salary was very high, and half of the salary was paid in advance immediately. The first disadvantage was that it was located in a remote village, and the second was to meet the customers' wives' "hobbies" in dress and hairstyle. "It seemed to me that I had never met so fascinating and so thoughtful aman. As I was already in debt to my tradesmen, the advance was a great convenience..." said Miss Hunter. However, during the whole conversation, Miss Hunter always felt that some places were unnatural—or not normal (suspicious), so she decided to learn more about the situation before making a decision. In other words, Miss Hunter had doubts about the work and was at a loss. Therefore, she asked Holmes for help.

Holmes could not explain why for a moment because he had no material information. As the saying goes, a skillful woman cannot make bricks without straw.

Miss Hunter speculated: Lucas seemed to be a very kind and good-natured person. Could it be that his wife is crazy? He would take various measures to satisfy her hobby and prevent her from being sent to a mental hospital due to her nervous attack.

Holmes said, this might be the case. However, Holmes also had a premonition that" in any case, it is not a good family for a young lady. "He basically agreed with Miss Hunter's speculation, but also had a bad feeling. Presumption and intuition do not belong to the same category. The former refers to the pre perception of the future, and the latter refers to the thinking that is currently running.

Finally, Miss Hunter made an agreement with Holmes and Watson to invite them to Winchester when she thought it was necessary.

Holmes said: "I have devised seven separate explanations, each of which would cover the facts as far as we know them. But which of these is correct can only be determined by the fresh information which we shall no doubt find waiting for us."

What does it mean? That is to say, Holmes once had seven different speculations (specifically, which seven are not introduced in the works, but may refer to "many" falsely), each based on the known facts at that time, but it is impossible to determine which is correct or not. Only when new information comes out can we determine which speculation is correct or not. As has been introduced previously, the correctness of intuitive results depends on logical tests and facts.

When they were invited to Winchester and listened to Miss Hunter's detailed introduction, Holmes began to speculate about this matter:

First, Miss Hunter was hired to go to Lucas' to pretend to be someone, and that person was probably imprisoned in a dark room;

Second, the imprisoned person is Miss Alice, the so-called daughter of Lucas in the United States;

Third, Miss Hunter was chosen because her height, figure and hair color were the same as Alice's;

Fourth, the man looking in on the road is Alice's boyfriend or fiance;

Fifth, the dog was released at night to prevent the man from contacting her.

The detailed, timely and accurate information laid the foundation for Holmes to speculate correctly and pointed out the direction for solving the mystery of hiring Miss Hunter with high salary.

THE MEMOIRS OF SHERLOCK HOLMES

1. Siver Blaze

Holmes Speculated A Lot in the Investigation of This Case:

"It is one of those cases where the art of the reasoner should be used rather for the sifting of details than for the acquiring of fresh evidence.The tragedy has been so uncommon, so complete, and of such personal importance to so many people that we are suffering from a plethora of surmise, conjecture, and hypothesis."

"My friend Dr. Watson made that suggestion to me as we came down.If so, it would tell against this man Simpson."

"A long shot, Watson, a very long shot," said he, pinching my arm."Gregory, let me recommend to your attention this singular epidemic among the sheep. Drive on, coachman!"

"My final shot was, I confess, a very long one. It struck me that so astute a man as Straker would not undertake this delicate tendon-nicking without a little practise. What could he practise on? My eyes fell upon the sheep, and I asked a question which, rather to my surprise, showed that my surmise was correct."

Holmes used a lot of speculations in this case, which played a very good role in speculating about the case and successfully solving the case.

2. The Yellow Face

A. Holmes' Intuition Show (No. 12):

A seemingly ordinary pipe left by the customer, Holmes observed it and thought it was the customer's very precious pipe.

"How do you know that he values it highly?" Watson asked.

Holmes reasoned:"Well, I should put the original cost of the pipe at seven and sixpence.Now it has, you see, been twice mended, once in the wooden stem and once in the amber. Each of these mends, done, as you observe, with silver bands, must have cost more than the pipe did originally. The man must value the pipe highly when he prefers to patch it up rather than buy a new one with the same money."

Holmes also believed: "The owner is obviously a muscular man, left-handed, with an excellent set of teeth, careless in his habits, and with no need to practise economy." was "a strong man, a left-handed man, a good tooth, careless, and rich."

Holmes then reasoned: The cigarette holder was bitten through, indicating that he was strong and had neat teeth; the right side of the pipe has been burnt, which is caused by left-handed people's habit of lighting the pipe on the oil lamp and gas burner; it means carelessness to leave your favorite things outside; he smoked tobacco for 8p an ounce. With half the price, he could smoke first-class cigarettes. It shows that he is not worried about money.

B. Holmes' inaccurate intuition.

Although Holmes is the image representative of a detective, and his intuitive thinking is more outstanding and pure, it does not mean that he did not stumble and lose his intuition, did not "doze" or make "mistakes". This is the Sherlock Holmes in the world. This is the place where the characters of Sherlock Holmes are vivid, flesh and blood, amiable, trustworthy and respectable.In "The Five Orange Pips," Holmes admitted that "I have been beaten four times—three times by men, and once by a woman." he has failed four times—three times to several men and one time to a woman." In this work, Holmes is defeated by "overconfidence".

Holmes made some "inferences" about the illness and emotional entanglement of Monroe's wife's ex husband, and asked Watson to make an evaluation. However, Watson believes that this is not a deduction, "it is purely speculation.". Watson's understanding is correct. Because "inference" is the result of reasoning, accurate and definite, and clearly the result of logical thinking. Speculation, as a form of intuition, is speculation based on certain clues. Its conclusions have great uncertainty, and its accuracy varies from person to person and from event to event. It requires constant comparison and correction with new information to obtain more accurate results. The result that Holmes guessed here is far from the truth. Let Holmes in front of Iron Powder Watson was shocked and embarrassed.

The sensitivity of intuition is often talked about and praised by people, which has its obvious advantages, but also has shortcomings. If they are not well mastered and used, they are prone to deviation and go astray.Intuitive thinking has four "incorrigible" and insurmountable "hard wounds", including Sherlock Holmes, a world-class detective.It is easy to be conceited and overconfident, which often occurs after one or two correct intuitions, and then becomes complacent and dizzy with profits, and the final result may be chicken feathers. We call it the conceited type. Holmes' guess in this work is a typical example. This is one of them.The second is that it is difficult to grasp the sharpness. If you are not careful, you may lose it too much. If you are too careful, you may also lose it too much, which will bring side effects. "Seeing the wind is rain", "chasing shadows" and so on are too sensitive or even neurotic. In the Last Case, Holmes became overly sensitive in order to avoid being tracked by the criminal gang leader Moriarty (detailed introduction later). We call it neurotic.Third, there is also a fatal disadvantage, which is particularly narcissistic. It is easy to be self-centered. In other words, subjectivity is very strong. Of course, it is understandable, because a large part of intuition is based on personal experience and social experience. We call it self righteous.Fourth, unique to emperors or power obsessed bosses, they use and doubt their deputies and subordinates, especially those who hold important power and positions. They often wonder whether they are still loyal to themselves and whether they are ready to form a party and engage in private affairs instead. As a result, it is either credulous and slanderous or deliberately trying to find out the truth, which creates great psychological pressure on the deputies and subordinates. Therefore, when things are extreme, they will turn against each other.It is not uncommon for these people to be betrayed by others.

C. Mr. Monroe's doubts about his wife Effie:

Monroe's wife was a widow and rich woman. After her ex husband died, she left a lot of property. From then on, she hated the United States and returned to England to live with her unmarried aunt. Six months later, Monroe and she fell in love at first sight, and got married a few weeks later. Monroe was a businessman, and he had a good income every year. After marriage, the wife transferred all her ex husband's inheritance to Monroe. Therefore, they lived a carefree life and their emotions were like glue. However, the good times didn't last long. About six weeks ago, she was quite different. She often sneaked into the neighborhood at night and asked some strange questions————

1. Wife Effie wanted 100 pounds. What was the purpose? Effie said it would take several days to tell. Doubts had increased without being answered.

2. Who was the strange face of the villa? Man or woman? He decided to visit. Suspicions continued to grow, and the strange man and the rude girl neighbor kept haunting him all night.

3. What was his wife going out with a hood at three in the morning for? It was fruitless to try to solve the doubts, and the doubts continued to strengthen.

4. "Where in the world have you been, Effie?" His wife turned pale and added new doubts to him.

5. "Where have you been?" His wife explained that the air in the room was dull and she stood outside for a few minutes.

6. Obvious lies! What was she hiding? Where did she go? Thousands of malicious doubts grew in his heart.

7. When passing the villa, he saw his wife coming out, and said, "I'm absolutely sure you came here yesterday. Who are these people? You came to see them at midnight?" Monroe wanted to go in and find out, but his wife persuaded him. When doubts are blocked, new doubts emerge.

8. When I left the villa, I saw strange faces looking at us: What's the relationship between my wife and the strange man? What is the relationship between my wife and that rude woman? Doubts of overlapping can never be solved, and the mood can never be calm.

9. One day, when he came home early, his wife was not at home. "My mind was instantly filled with suspicion." The maid went to the villa to inform his wife, and Monroe rushed into the villa to unlock the secret. But the room was empty, only a full body picture of his wife. At this time, "...all my suspicions rose into a fierce, bitter..."

Monroe decided to visit Holmes in order to solve the mystery.

One after another, the questioning type, which promotes the flames, is closely linked and fascinating. It not only reflects Monroe's mood, but also makes the story of the work ups and downs. It can't help but play a very good suspense effect.

3. The Stock-broker's Clerk

A. Holmes' Intuition Show (No. 13):

Holmes came to Watson's clinic, narrowed his sharp eyes, looked at Watson and said, "I perceive that you have been unwell lately."

"And from what?" asked Watson.

"From your slippers."

Then Holmes spread his wings of reasoning:

"Your slippers are new," he said. "You could not have had them more than a few weeks. The soles which you are at this moment presenting to me are slightly scorched. For a moment I thought they might have got wet and been burned in the drying. But near the instep there is a small circular wafer of paper with the shopman's hieroglyphics upon it. Damp would of course have removed this. You had, then, been sitting with your feet outstretched to the fire, which a man would hardly do even in so wet a June as this if he were in his full health."

B. Holmes' Intuition Show (No. 14):

At the invitation of Holmes, Watson went to help investigate the case and asked the doctor in the neighbor's clinic to look after his own clinic. Holmes said, "Ah! then you got hold of the best of the two."

"I think I did. But how do you know?" asked Watson.

Holmes said: "By the steps, my boy. Yours are worn three inches deeper than his."

Only when observation is meticulous, can intuition have penetrating effect.

4. The "Gloria Scott"

Holmes' Intuition Show (No. 15):

Old Trevor heard that his son, young Trevor, introduced that Holmes was good at observation (intuition) and reasoning. He thought that he was exaggerating, so he wanted to test him face to face to see if Holmes could see something in him. Then there was a progressive intuition show of Holmes:

Holmes said: "I might suggest that you have gone about in fear of some personal attack within the last twelvemonth."

The laugh faded from Trevor's lips, and he stared at Holmes in great surprise: "...I have no idea how you know it."

Holmes said: "You have a very handsome stick.By the inscription I observed that you had not had it more than a year. But you have taken some pains to bore the head of it and pour melted lead into the hole so as to make it a formidable weapon. I argued that you would not take such precautions unless you had some danger to fear."

"Anything else?" asked Trevor.

Holmes said, when you were young, you liked boxing.

Trevor agreed and asked how he knew.

"It is your ears. They have the peculiar flattening and thickening which marks the boxing man."

You have calluses in your hands. You have worked in mining for many years... You have been to New Zealand... You have visited Japan.

Trevor admitted one by one.

The most wonderful thing is that when Holmes said that he once had a very close relationship with a person, but now he wanted to forget him completely. The initials of that person's name were "J.A.", Trevor slowly stood up, stared at Holmes with strange and crazy eyes, and then fell forward unconscious.

After Trevor woke up, he couldn't wait to know the secret in his heart. How did Holmes know? How much did he know?

Holmes, however, drifted back and said that one day when we were in the boat, you rolled up your sleeves to catch fish. I saw that you had the word "J.A." stabbed at the bend of your arm, but the strokes were vague. There were ink stains around the words, indicating that you tried to erase the words and completely forget them later.

Trevor said admiringly, your eyesight is so powerful!

5. The Musgrave Ritual

Guess (Speculation) to Solve the Mystery of Manor House of Hurlstone:

Holmes found three recent mysteries of his college classmate Musgrave's home, Manor House of Hurlstone.First, the senior housekeeper Brenton was severely punished by Musgrave for secretly reading Musgrave Ritual. On the third day, he disappeared mysteriously;second, Howells, the maid who had an affair with Brenton, also disappeared three days later;third, the contents of the Musgrave Ritual that Brenton secretly read are very strange and difficult to understand.

"These three riddles deeply attracted Holmes, and through overall understanding, 'I have been convinced that these are not isolated three riddles, but just a riddle. If I can correctly interpret the' Musgrave Ritual ', I will definitely be able to seize the clues and find out the truth about butler Brenton and maid Howells.'"

Through studying the heavenly book Musgrave Ritual, Holmes speculated that there should be an oak tree and an old elm tree in the manor.In the former, Holmes' guess had been confirmed by Musgrave. Holmes asked:Do you have an old elm?The latter was recalled by Musgrave. A few months ago, the housekeeper Brenton asked about the height of the old elm, which was knocked down by lightning ten years ago. That is to say, Holmes also guessed the old elm.

According to this speculation, Holmes finally found the passage paved with stone slabs. There was a cellar under the slabs. Many treasures were found in the cellar. Brenton, the housekeeper who had been missing for several days and died, was found here.

Then Holmes guessed:

Brenton knew that treasures were hidden under the manor through studying Masgrave Ritual, and he found the specific location accurately. When he found that the stone cover was too heavy to move, he found Howells, the maid who had been attracted to him, to help him.Only one person could enter the cellar. It must be Brenton who went in and handed the treasure to Howells.At this moment, the impetuous Welsh girl saw that the person who had betrayed her was in such a dangerous situation. Maybe he treated her much worse than we thought, and she felt a sense of resentment.Perhaps the wood supporting the slate suddenly slipped, and the slate fell, locking Brenton in the cellar, and she refused to save his life;or maybe she deliberately pushed the wood away and let the slate cover the cellar opening, making Brenton suffocate in the cellar. "Be that as it might, I seemed to see that woman's figure still clutching at her treasure trove and flying wildly up the winding stair, with her ears ringing perhaps with the muffled screams from behind her and with the drumming of frenzied hands against the slab of stone which was choking her faithless lover's life out."

"Here was the secret of her blanched face, her shaken nerves, her peals of hysterical laughter on the next morning." Since then, this woman had never been heard of, and she had fled to the ends of the world.

Guess is the combination of intuitive thinking and image thinking. "Guess" is speculation based on certain clues, and "think" is imagination based on certain clues, but its essence is still "guess", that is, the type of speculation.

6. The Reigate Puzzle

Importance of Overall Grasp Ability in Investigation:

"It is of the highest importance in the art of detection to be able to recognize, out of a number of facts, which are incidental and which vital.Otherwise your energy and attention must be dissipated instead of being concentrated. Now, in this case there was not the slightest doubt in my mind from the first that the key of the whole matter must be looked for in the scrap of paper in the dead man's hand."

Perhaps I am ignorant, but I think Holmes is probably the first person to consider the work of investigation as an art. No wonder he was always devoted to his work, crazy and intoxicated. At the same time, Holmes also emphasized the important role of the overall grasp ability in the investigation work.

"The most basic feature of human psychology is the wholeness that appears in conscious experience, and the wholeness is also the most significant feature of our intuitive thinking, which takes the object as a whole from the beginning of the cognitive process." ("Introduction to Personality Psychology" written by Gao Yuxiang)Therefore, it is an important function of intuitive thinking to accurately and quickly grasp, identify the primary and secondary, weight, advantages and disadvantages, and find out their essential characteristics from the complex phenomenon.

The crime scene is full of complicated clues. To find useful clues and determine the correct direction of investigation as soon as possible, investigators need to have a strong overall grasp and identification ability. The static scene can be grasped calmly, while for the rapidly changing investigation and arrest scene, the front-line commander or investigators must be quick to grasp the scene, or they will miss the opportunity.

How to develop overall grasping ability? Practice in daily life: after reading an article, quickly say the central idea or underline the central word; watch film and television works, preferably in foreign languages, and speculate on the theme while watching; when you see a person, describe it immediately his character traits. You can also sum up a few experiences or lessons from what you or others have encountered and heard. If you keep doing it for a long time, your overall grasping ability will be greatly improved.

Due to Sherlock Holmes' strong overall grasping ability, he directly hit the key of the case—the shredded paper, which held the "bull's nose" of the case, so the case was successfully detected.

7. The Crooked Man

Holmes' Intuition Show (No. 16):

Late one night, Holmes stayed at Watson's house and casually said:There was a repairman at home. Not the drains, I hope?

Watson said:"No, the gas."

Holmes explained:"Ah! He has left two nail-marks from his boot upon your linoleum just where the light strikes it."

Are you busy recently? Holmes asked again.

"Yes, I've had a busy day," Watson answered. "It may seem very foolish in your eyes," Watson added, "but really I don't know how you deduced it."

Holmes chuckled to himself. "I have the advantage of knowing your habits, my dear Watson," said Holmes. "When your round is a short one you walk, and when it is a long one you use a hansom. As I perceive that your boots, although used, are by no means dirty, I cannot doubt that you are at present busy enough to justify the hansom."

"Excellent!" Watson cried.

8. The Resident Patient

A. Holmes Guessed the "Mental Journey" Through
Micro Expressions and Micro Movements:

Watson thought Holmes was so absorbed in thinking that he could not speak, so he threw the newspaper aside and leaned back against the chair, lost in a brown study. At this time, Holmes spoke and interrupted Watson's thoughts.

"You are right, Watson," said Holmes. "It does seem a very preposterous way of settling a dispute."

It turned out that Holmes had been observing Watson, and to Watson's surprise, Holmes even knew what he was thinking at this moment!

"Most preposterous!" Watson exclaimed, how did he know this idea in my heart? "What is this, Holmes?" Watson couldn't help wondering.

Then Holmes recalled a past event to Watson, who expressed different views on it at that time.

"Oh, no!" Watson recalled.

"Perhaps not with your tongue, my dear Watson, but certainly with your eyebrows. So when I saw you throw down your paper and enter upon a train of thought, I was very happy to have the opportunity of reading it off, and eventually of breaking into it, as a proof that I had been in rapport with you."

Holmes also said: "The features are given to man as the means by which he shall express his emotions, and yours are faithful servants." "Your features, and especially your eyes."

Holmes could not help laughing when he saw Watson with a blank face.

So Holmes told him how to "see" his "mental journey" from his "micro expressions", "micro movements", especially his eyes:

1. The act of you dropping the newspaper has attracted my attention to you;
2. Then you sat there blankly for half a minute;
3. Then your eyes stared at your newly framed portrait of General Gordon;
4. From the change of your facial expression, I could see that you had started to think about things, but you don't think very far;
5. Then your eyes turned to the framed portrait of Henry Ward Beecher on the bookshelf;
6. Then you looked up at the wall and think that if this portrait was also equipped with a frame, it could be hung in the blank space of this wall and arranged with the Gordon portrait.
7. Then you concentrated on the portrait of Beecher, and your thoughts returned to Beecher, as if you were studying his character from his face.
8. Later, you no longer frowned, but continued to stare. Your face looked thoughtful, which showed that you were recalling the events that Beecher experienced. I was sure that you were reminded of his mission on behalf of the North during the civil war, because I remembered you were very angry about his experience (accurate intuition is based on understanding).
9. After a while, your eyes moved away from the portrait, and I thought your thoughts turned to the civil war again;
10. I found your lips tightly closed, your eyes bright, and your hands clenched. I was sure you were thinking about the bravery of both sides in this deadly battle;
11. However, your face became gloomy again, and you shook your head. You were thinking about the tragedy and horror of war, and the futility of killing and injuring many people;
12. Your hand slowly moved to your old scar and a smile appeared on your lips. I think you were thinking that such a solution to international problems is ridiculous.

"Absolutely!" said I. "And now that you have explained it, I confess that I am as amazed as before."

In the above observations, Holmes mainly involved people's movements, eyes, expressions, as well as looks, voices, and abnormal phenomena, etc. These vivid information that are closely related to people's daily life are particularly "preferred" and "loved" "food" by intuitive thinking.

Intuition is the oldest and most primitive human thinking. In the ancient times with low productivity, in order to survive, human beings had to hunt and pick wild fruits to satisfy their hunger, and resist the invasion of natural disasters and wild animals, so they had to communicate and cooperate. Because there were no words and languages at that time, human expressions and body movements became the most direct and acceptable medium for everyone to express their thoughts.Therefore, intuitive thinking, which was closely related to human visual system, had important functions and was becoming more and more mature and perfect in daily work and life. At the same time, how to correctly interpret people's expressions and actions had also become an important task of intuitive thinking.

Intuition is not only closely related to people's daily life, but also to investigation. If it is said that investigation emerges as the times require when crime occurs, then intuition goes hand in hand with investigation. In the unknown era when crime was born, there was no surveillance, no fingerprint extraction technology, no DNA, and no assistance from big data and other investigative technologies. The investigation and solving of cases depended more on the intuitive thinking of law enforcement officers or detectives. In other words, intuitive thinking is the most primitive and important weapon for law enforcement or detectives to investigate and solve cases. The strength or weakness of their intuitive thinking ability directly determines the level of detection and solving. Even with the rapid development of science and technology today, intuitive thinking still plays an important role in investigation and continues to play a leading role, such as the ability to use, identify and interpret big data when viewing big data, etc. Therefore, it is of great practical significance to explore, study and summarize the role of intuitive thinking in investigation.

In China's Song Dynasty's *Analysis and Reflection of Cases* (Zheng Ke, 8 Volumes, 395 Cases), and the contemporary *Supplement to Analysis and Reflection of Cases* (Editor-in-Chief Chen Zhong, 6 Volumes, 719 cases), a large number of classic intuitive investigation cases are recorded. These cases particularly clearly reflect the important role of intuitive thinking in investigation, and provide us with rich and detailed data for the study of intuitive investigative thinking.

The ability of intuition is to catch the unusual in ordinary people's seemingly ordinary through the instantaneous changes of people's external appearance. This ability is particularly important for detectives. Why can we find problems in an inconspicuous look of people? Because there is a lot of content hidden in people's looks! How to discover and accurately interpret these contents is worthy of our study and discussion.

According to the research of an American psychologist, expression and action account for 55% of the results of information exchange, while non-verbal total accounts for 93%. Most of the information that people can effectively communicate face to face is nonverbal information. All body movements and behaviors of people convey information.

Guiguzi said: "The desire in the heart can be shaped by the external appearance. Therefore, you can know the desire in other people's hearts by observing their faces from time to time."

Some modern researchers believe that sitting posture reveals people's psychological trends; standing posture reveals one's personality; walking posture can be described as the words revealed under your feet; fist waving is the declaration of power; Gestures convey the voice of the soul. Habitual actions reflect human personality and behavioral characteristics.

In 1996, President Clinton declared in public and under oath that "I didn't have sex with that woman (Lewinsky)." It took only five seconds to speak, but his eyes blinked four times; when speaking, stretch out the right index finger to emphasize the content but in the opposite direction; wrinkles on the forehead disappeared quickly after the words were said. People speculated that Clinton told a lie based on his actions, which later proved to be true.

People often say that the eyes are the windows and mirrors of the soul. Through the fleeting eyes, the secret of human heart can be captured. Of course, you must have strong observation and find more details to touch your intuitive thinking, otherwise, you can't interpret, or even turn a blind eye.

Mencius believed that good and evil can be seen from the eyes:There is nothing better in a man's body that exists inside but appears outside than his eyes. The eyes cannot hide a man's ugly soul. If the heart is right, the eyes will be bright; if the heart is not right, the eyes will be dark. When listening to a man, observe his eyes. Where can his good and evil hide?

Folk sayings are similar to Mencius' view. They believe that people who are kind and simple have open and serene eyes; those who are narrow-minded and selfish have cunning and dark eyes; those who are not fond of wealth or power have straight and strong eyes; those who change their minds and see the rudder of the wind have their eyes wandering and erratic.

A famous German psychologist said that eyes are the best tool to understand a person.

Psychologists' research shows that 83% of the information conveyed to the human mind comes from the eyes, 11% from the ears and 6% from other organs. Although there were no such research results in Holmes' time, capturing people's psychological activities through eyes (gods) was an important way for people at all times and in all countries.

It can be seen that the position of the eyes in the sensory organs; it can be seen that the eyes have rich connotations!

The expressions or the looks of the eyes are existing and changing all the time for everyone except sleeping. It depends on your ability to capture them and interpret them correctly. For the former, observation can help you, while for the latter, you can only rely on intuitive thinking.

B. Holmes' Intuition Show (No.17):

"Hum! A doctor's—general practitioner, I perceive," said Holmes.

Watson knew that Holmes was good at observation and reasoning, and he was influenced by what he saw and heard, so he naturally learned something more or less. Then he did not ask Holmes how he saw it, but made his own reasoning through observation:

There was a wicker basket hanging under the lamp in the car, which contained a variety of medical devices. Holmes made a quick judgment based on the types and conditions of these medical devices.

9. The Greek Interpreter

Holmes and his brother's intuition show (No. 18):

Holmes is a very confident person. He thinks his detective ability, especially his observation, intuition and reasoning ability, is unparalleled.In "A Study of Scarlet," Watson sincerely praised Holmes' detective ability and compared him with Du Ban, a detective in the works of his idol writer Edgar Allan Poe. Unexpectedly, he aroused Holmes' antipathy.Sherlock Holmes rose and lit his pipe. "No doubt you think that you are complimenting me in comparing me to Dupin," he observed. "Now, in my opinion, Dupin was a very inferior fellow. That trick of his of breaking in on his friends' thoughts with an apropos remark after a quarter of an hour's silence is really very showy and superficial. He had some analytical genius, no doubt; but he was by no means such a phenomenon as Poe appeared to imagine."

Watson, who met with a rebuke, turned to test Holmes' views on another of his detective idols.

"Have you read Gaboriau's works?" Watson asked. "Does Lecoq come up to your idea of a detective?"

Sherlock Holmes sniffed sardonically. "Lecoq was a miserable bungler," he said, in an angry voice; "he had only one thing to recommend him, and that was his energy. That book made me positively ill. The question was how to identify an unknown prisoner. I could have done it in twenty-four hours. Lecoq took six months or so. It might be made a textbook for detectives to teach them what to avoid."

Watson was embarrassed and angry when he heard Holmes say that the two characters he admired were worthless. "This fellow may be very clever," Watson said to myself, "but he is certainly very conceited."

However, Holmes thought that his brother, Michael Roft, was better at observation—intuition—reasoning than him, except that he was not a detective. What's the truth? Let's see Holmes and his brother's intuition show:

They sat by the window of a club.

"To anyone who wishes to study mankind this is the spot," said Mycroft. "Look at the magnificent types! Look at these two men who are coming towards us, for example."

"The billiard-marker and the other?"

"Precisely. What do you make of the other?"

The two men had stopped opposite the window. Some chalk marks over the waistcoat pocket were the only signs of billiards which I could see in one of them. The other was a very small, dark fellow, with his hat pushed back and several packages under his arm.

"An old soldier, I perceive," said Sherlock.}He is a soldier, not an ordinary soldier, with a powerful look and sun exposed skin.

"And very recently discharged," remarked the brother.}He still wore the artillery boots.

"Served in India, I see."}He has just returned from India.

"And a non-commissioned officer."}Mycroft answered Sherlock, "He is not an ordinary soldier."

"Royal Artillery, I fancy," said Sherlock.}He didn't walk like a cavalry, but he wore a hat askew, which could be seen from the light skin on one side of his eyebrow. His weight does not meet the requirements of an engineer, so he is said to be an artillery.

"And a widower."}He explained later.

"But with a child."}It was Sherlock's speculation.

"Children, my dear boy, children." Mycroft corrected Sherlock's speculation with his own.

"Surely," answered Holmes.}Sherlock agreed to his brother's speculation.

Mycroft said:"...his complete mourning shows..."}That means he lost someone. From the things he bought, he looked like a widower. A rattle shows that a child is very young. A comic book shows that he still misses another child.

From the above dialogue, it can be seen that Mycroft is indeed better than Shylock in observation—intuition—reasoning.

In addition, Holmes said that when Edgar Allan Poe's Du Ban solved the problem for others in "A Study in Scarlet," ""...Dupin was a very inferior fellow. That trick of his of breaking in on his friends' thoughts with an apropos remark after a quarter of an hour's silence is really very showy and superficial..." This situation of Du Ban is probably logical thinking rather than intuitive thinking, because most of the results of intuitive thinking flash out on the premise of "no thinking", which is thinking directly from phenomenon to result. To demonstrate whether the conclusion is right or not, it takes a certain amount of time for logical deduction.

10. The Naval Treaty

A. Holmes' Intuition Show (No. 19):

Percy is a school-fellow of Watson. He serves in the Ministry of Foreign Affairs and his uncle is the Foreign Minister. He works hard and has a bright future.Moreover, he will marry beautiful Miss Anne in the near future.However, at this moment, an unfortunate event happened to his young head. A secret document that the foreign minister gave him to copy disappeared a moment after he left the office. For this reason, he was seriously ill and never recovered. While reporting to the police, he also wanted to invite Holmes to investigate through Watson.After receiving the letter, Watson attached great importance to it and came to Baker Street to ask Holmes to solve the case. He handed Percy's letter and Holmes watched intently.

"It does not tell us very much, does it?" Holmes remarked.

"Hardly anything."

"And yet the writing is of interest."

"But the writing is not his own."

"Precisely. It is a woman's."

"A man's surely," Watson cried.

"No, a woman's, and a woman of rare character."

Then Holmes explained: From the beginning of the investigation, I knew that your client had a close relationship with a woman who had a distinctive personality. I'm interested in this case. We can go to Woking immediately to see your unfortunate diplomat school-fellow and the woman who wrote this letter on his behalf. It turned out that the letter was written by Anne, the fiancee of diplomat Percy, and she was indeed a girl with strong character.

B. Holmes' Intuition Show (No. 20):

When Holmes and Watson arrived in Woking, they were warmly received by a rather sturdy man who was nearly forty years old, with rosy cheeks, cheerful eyes. He gave the impression of a straightforward and innocent urchin.

Holmes asked:"I perceive that you are not yourself a member of the family."

Our acquaintance looked surprised, and then, glancing down, he began to laugh.

"Of course you saw the J H monogram on my locket," said he. "For a moment I thought you had done something clever. Joseph Harrison is my name, and as Percy is to marry my sister Annie I shall at least be a relation by marriage.."

C. Interpretation of "Seven".

There is a numeral "seven" in the whole "Sherlock Holmes" for four times. Is it real or empty?

"Do you see any clues?"

"You have provided me with seven clues, but of course I must examine them before I can judge their value."

In this article, the author does not explain which "seven clues" are, and the author is unable to find out these "seven clues".

"The Abbey Grange":"Hopkins has called me in seven times, and on each occasion his summons has been entirely justified," said Holmes.

"The Copper Beeches":"I have devised seven separate explanations, each of which would cover the facts as far as we know them."

"The Missing Three-Quarter": "I had seven different schemes for getting a glimpse of that telegram, but I could hardly hope to succeed the very first time."

In the above works, there is no specific reference to "seven times" and "seven kinds", and the author has not found out the relevant content. Therefore, we can understand that the numerals "seven" mentioned above are empty and probably local colloquial expressions. Just like the numbers in our oral language: "I've told this thing a hundred times", etc.

D. Holmes' Intuitive Investigation:

The secret documents that Percy transcribed in the office of the Foreign Ministry were mysteriously missing. There was no hiding place in the office or corridor. The man must have come in from outside. Although it was a rainy night, there were no wet footprints left.

"...then it is exceedingly probable that he came in a cab. Yes, I think that we may safely deduce a cab."

After Holmes and Watson came to Woking again, Percy told the thrilling scene of the burglar in his room last night. Because of his poor health, he did not pursue. He shouted, first Joseph came, and then he woke the others. Because of the dry weather, Joseph and the groom only found blurred footprints outside the window, and the wooden fence on the roadside broke the railing tip when they climbed over. Holmes suggested going to look around the house, but asked Miss Harrison not to go and to stay in the room.

Holmes asked, "Why did the thief choose this room? The large windows in the living room and dining room should be more attractive to him."

Joseph said, "Those windows can be seen clearly from the road."

Holmes asked again, "There is a door here. He can try it here."

Joseph said, "This is the side door for businessmen to enter and exit. It is locked at night."

Holmes asked Percy, "Do you have gold and silver tableware or other valuables in your house?"

Percy said no. Holmes put his hands into his pockets and walked around the house with an expression he had never seen before. Then he asked Joseph: I heard that you found a wooden railing broken by someone. Joseph took everyone over. Holmes looked carefully and said: This trace looks old, doesn't it? Joseph said awkwardly: Ah, maybe it is!—At this moment, Holmes has a more mature speculation about the theft —It happened at home and occur internally.

Holmes hurried back to the room and said very seriously to Miss Harrison, "You must stay here all day and don't leave if anything happens.". Before going to bed, lock the door from outside and take the key yourself. The young lady agreed in surprise and doubt. Then Holmes took Percy back to London. After Watson and Percy got on the train, Holmes suddenly said that he would stay in Woking and agreed to go back to London for breakfast the next morning. This makes them puzzled.

The next morning, Holmes returned with injury as promised and put the recovered secret documents on the table. Percy fainted because of excessive excitement. It turned out that the thief was his future brother-in-law Joseph Harrison.

Holmes said of Joseph:"Hum! I am afraid Joseph's character is a rather deeper and more dangerous one than one might judge from his appearance. From what I have heard from him this morning, I gather that he has lost heavily in dabbling with stocks, and that he is ready to do anything on earth to better his fortunes. Being an absolutely selfish man, when a chance presents itself he did not allow either his sister's happiness or your reputation to hold his hand. "This also reminds people that the appearance is like a black cloth in the hands of a magician, and there is something magical behind it that you cannot imagine. The image of "a straightforward and innocent urchin" does not necessarily mean that the inner heart is also "straightforward and innocent".

Finally, Holmes made a closing statement: the main difficulty of this case is that there are too many clues.The vital clues were obscured by irrelevant signs. There are so many facts in front of us that we can only choose the necessary ones and string them in order to attach importance to all aspects of this strange chain of events.The reason why I began to doubt Joseph was that you planned to go back to Wokin with Joseph on the night of the theft. I naturally thought that he would come to you. He should be familiar with the Foreign Ministry.Later, on the night when no one stayed with you, someone was eager to steal from your bedroom.I think the secret documents should be hidden in your bedroom, because Joseph stayed there temporarily before. He has this convenience.You once said how Joseph moved out of your bedroom when you returned to the bedroom with the doctor that day. "At that time, my suspicion (doubt type) turned into affirmation (conclusion type)." Although I knew for a long time that nine out of ten documents were hidden in the bedroom, I was reluctant to search for it. I will let him take it out of his hiding place, which will save me a lot of trouble.

11. The Final Problem

福尔摩斯的直觉场与反直觉场:

Holmes' Intuition Field and Anti Intuition Field:

Holmes was tracked for revenge and his life was threatened because he was investigating a criminal group headed by Professor Moriarty. So Holmes took a series of anti intuitive measures.

Anti intuition field is a phenomenon corresponding to intuition field and a pair of contradictions. Before introducing the intuitionistic field and anti intuitionistic field, we should first introduce the field and observation field.

Field, a basic form of the existence of matter, has energy, momentum and mass, and can transfer the interaction between objects, such as electric field, magnetic field, gravitational field and gas field. In our body, cells are always digesting nutrients through chemical action to generate energy, supply the growth of body and mind, and make them always have endless vitality. As long as your body is healthy, the energy factory in your body will not stop running. Under the guidance of this powerful physiological energy, there is always a magnetic field in our body. The research of California Institute of Technology in the United States confirmed that the human brain can not only sense magnetic fields, but also make strong responses to changes in magnetic fields. Others believe that the electromagnetic field in and around the body will expand and change before and after intuition appears.

Therefore, there is a field between us. You radiate your field and accept others' field all the time.

Observation field is a purposeful and planned perceptual activity of two or more hostile parties, which is mainly visual, but not only visual, but also includes active thinking participation; its purpose is to watch and perceive the details and clues of the other party as much as possible in a specific time, space and form to lay a solid foundation for starting intuition. The reverse observation field is the opposite. The observation of a single individual cannot become a field.

John Douglas, the top American criminal personality portrait expert, said "If I were a murderer, I would go out every day to look for prey. Just like a documentary that reflects nature, there is a lion standing on the plains of Africa. It finds thousands of antelopes in the pond. From the eyes of this well-trained lion, we can see that it can observe the weakness of an antelope in the flock and may eventually become its food. If I walk into the game room of a shopping center and see more than 50 children playing games, I must find out which of the more than 50 children is easy to attack and may become a victim. I must observe and capture clues from the child's clothes, gestures, expressions and postures, and it must be done in an instant. Once I have made a decision, once I want to start, I must figure out how to get the child out of the game hall and shopping center quietly and quietly. Because his or her parents are probably in the nearby shop, I can't make any mistakes."

Here, "I" and more than 50 children and their parents are an observation field. If "I" and more than 50 children are direct observation fields, then "I" and more than 50 parents of "absent" and "unseen" children are indirect observation fields.

Like the observation field, the intuition field is also an intentional and planned activity involving both or more hostile parties. The difference is that it is an indirect reflection of the objective world and belongs to the level of thinking. It can penetrate and grasp the essence of things through various phenomena observed.

Observation—The intuition field is often intertwined, and it is difficult to divide it absolutely. In "The Engineer's Thumb," the victim engineer and the perpetrator colonel are an observation—intuition field.

The victim, Hasselly, was a hydraulic engineer. After inheriting a considerable inheritance from his father, he opened a company in Victoria Street. In the past two years, the company has been operating in a dismal and disheartened manner. All of a sudden, he also got lucky. A big customer came to the store, and the name of Colonel Lysander Stark was printed on his business card.

The colonel was of medium to high stature and extremely thin. His whole face was thin, except for his nose and chin. The skin of his cheeks was tight on the protruding cheekbones. However, his haggard appearance seems to be born, rather than due to disease, because he has bright eyes, brisk steps and free manners—the colonel gives an ugly image to engineers;

The colonel first paid a compliment to the engineer, which made him "feel elated." The engineer asked, "Who told me so well?" —The engineer really enjoyed the compliments of others;

"Maybe I'd better not tell you at present. I heard from the same source that you are both an orphan and a bachelor, and live alone in London."—The colonel understands and verifies the engineer's life experience;

"I can't see that these have anything to do with my business ability."—The engineer was a little confused;

"Undoubtedly so. But you will find that all I say is really to the point.I have a professional commission for you, but absolute secrecy is quite essential–absolute secrecy, you understand, and of course we may expect that more from a man who is alone than from one who lives in the bosom of his family."—The colonel seemed to be clearing his doubts;

"If I promise to keep a secret, said I, you may absolutely depend upon my doing so." "He looked very hard at me as I spoke, and it seemed to me that I had never seen so suspicious and questioning an eye."—The engineer saw the "suspicion" in the colonel's eyes—the colonel's intuition field leaked (A detailed introduction will follow);

The colonel said: "Absolute and complete silence before, during, and after? No reference to the matter at all, either in word or writing?" "Very good." He suddenly sprang up, and darting like lightning acros the room he flung open the door. The passage outside was empty. "That's all right," said he, coming back. "I know the clerks are sometimes curious as to their master's affairs. Now we can talk in safety." He drew up his chair very close to mine and began to stare at me again with the same questioning and thoughtful look.—The colonel is suspicious not only in words but also in deeds;

"A feeling of repulsion, and of something akin to fear had begun to rise within me at the strange antics of this fleshless man."—Even his dread of losing a client could not restrain him from showing his impatience.

The colonel said that the job was to play with the hydraulic press for an hour or so every night. The work was very easy, but the remuneration was very generous.— The engineers were not alert to money, and the previous doubts were immediately dispelled;

The working place was a little far away, and the engineer was asked to go at eleven o'clock that night. It takes a train and the colonel picks him up in a carriage. The colonel said, "Still, of course, if you would like to draw out of the business, there is plenty of time to do so."

"I thought of the fifty guineas, and of how very useful they would be to me. 'Not at all,' said I, 'I shall be very happy to accommodate myself to your wishes. I should like, however, to understand a little more clearly what it is that you wish me to do.'—The engineer was happy and worried;

"Quite so. It is very natural that the pledge of secrecy which we have exacted from you should have aroused your curiosity. I have no wish to commit you to anything without your having it all laid before you. Isuppose that we are absolutely safe from eavesdroppers?"—The colonel took the initiative to "dispel doubts", further trapping the engineers, and at the same time pretending to be mysterious;

"You are probably aware that fuller's-earth is a valuable product, and that it is only found in one or two places in England?" So he made up a story about the secret discovery of bleach in the land they bought. The engineer said: "The only point which I could not quite understand was what use you could make of a hydraulic press in excavating fuller's-earth, which, as I understand, is dug out like gravel from a pit." The colonel continued to lie:We have our own process. We compress the earth into bricks, so as to remove them without revealing what they are.But that is a mere detail. I have taken you fully into my confidence now, Mr. Hatherley, and I have shown you how I trust you.I shall expect you, then, at Eyford at 11:15.

The engineer said: "I shall certainly be there." The colonel stressed again: "And not a word to a soul." At last, the colonel looked at the engineer with suspicion for a long time, then shook his hand. The colonel hurried out of the room—he waited for the fish to bite.

When the engineer calmed down and considered the matter comprehensively, he had mixed feelings: happily, the colonel's remuneration was at least ten times what he asked for, and it was likely to bring some other business; sadly, the customer's face and behavior gave him a very unpleasant impression. Besides, the explanation of bleach soil was not enough to explain the necessity of going late at night, nor why he was so worried about talking about the job to others.Finally, driven by interests, the engineer put all doubts and fears behind him and drove to Paddington as scheduled, almost on a road of no return. The engineer who narrowly escaped death found Holmes, and then revealed the real secret behind the intuition field, the observation staged by the engineer and the colonel.

A Qingsao, Diao Deyi and Hu Chuankui in the Peking Opera "Battle of Wisdom" are an intuition field.Although Hu Chuankui was a "straw bag", he also "saw" Diao Deyi's suspicious eyes on A Qingsao, the "savior". He felt that he had no face, and thought, "This little Diao doesn't talk about face at all!" He even scolded, "What kind of tricks did Diao Deyi do?" And Diao Deyi seemed to ignore it completely, and continued to fight with A Qingsao to try her out.A Qingsao did not show weakness and took it easy. Therefore, one is "I will visit her around the clock", and the other is "I must guard against him by observing what he says and looks like." Finally, with her outstanding intuitive ability and good psychological quality, A Qingsao won the "field" victory.

Therefore, intuition field is a material form objectively existing, which exists in the form of bilateral symmetry, multiple points and multiple lines, and no dead angle in all directions in a specific environment and space-time.It is difficult for ordinary people to "see" this scene, but people with keen observation and strong intuitive thinking ability can "see" his existence.In a word, the intuitive field is the place where observation and observation, intuitive thinking and intuitive thinking compete.The suspect detectives are wondering: what the suspect is thinking, what he will do, what is the meaning of this word and deed, and what should I do? The suspect is pondering against the detectives: what are they thinking, what will they do next, what is the meaning of these words and deeds, and how should I deal with them? This is a static intuition field and anti intuition field.

On the one hand, the intuition field should fully rely on and mobilize the keen intuition of detectives to find, detect and capture the intuition field that suspect diverge and leak out and make corresponding responses through the complicated, fragmented, unstable and fleeting phenomena; On the other hand, it is also necessary to ensure that the detectives' own intuition field cannot be disclosed, otherwise, they may fall short of success or even be doomed.

In this work, Holmes believes that there is a dangerous intuition field enveloping him from the following abnormal events:

At noon one day, he went to Oxford Street to deal with some affairs. Just passing the corner of the intersection from Bentink Street to Welbeck Street, a two horse van rushed towards him like lightning. He jumped onto the sidewalk in a hurry and survived at the critical moment. The van raced through Marley Lane in an instant. After this incident, he began to walk on the sidewalk, but when he reached Vail Street, a brick suddenly fell from the roof and was smashed in front of him. He called the police and checked the place. The roof was piled with stone slabs and bricks for house repair. The police said that the wind had blown a brick off. However, Holmes knew very well that the above "accident" was not accidental, but someone wanted to harm him but could not get proof. Just now, when he came to Watson's house, he was attacked by a mob with a big stick. He hit the front teeth of the mob with his fist and scratched his knuckles. Although the police detained the mob, they could never find out the relationship between him and Mauriati.

Anti intuition field refers to the speech and behavior of the intuition field, in which one party purposefully and intentionally creates false images and conceals the truth from the other, so as to confuse the truth with the false, make it difficult to distinguish the true from the false, interfere with the audio-visual, and mislead the observation. Detectives and detectives can use it.

In "The Sign of Four," Holmes used the police's mistake to capture all of them as a cover: Jones's action is beneficial to us. Because his opinion is published in the newspaper every day, the bandits will think that everyone is investigating in the wrong direction, and they can live in peace for a while. Holmes thus gained valuable time for himself to find the whereabouts of the gas ship and hunt down the real suspects.

In order to prevent Mauriati, the leader of the high IQ criminal group, from stalking and harming, Holmes also showed his counter intuitive skills as a high IQ detective.

When he came to Watson's house, he first closed the shutters and left by turning over the back wall instead of the front door. He was going to leave England with Watson to hide from the edge, warned Watson that his luggage must not be marked with the destination, and sent it to Victoria Station through a reliable person that night. You should hire a two wheeled carriage the next morning, but don't hire the first and second carriages that take the initiative to get business. After jumping into the carriage, you write an address on a note to the coachman. It says that you are to the end of Strand, Lauser Street, and tell him not to lose the note. Pay the fare in advance. As soon as your car stops, cross the street and arrive at the other end of the street at 9:15. You will see a four wheeled sedan car waiting at the street side. The driver, the coachman dressed up by Sherlock

Holmes' brother, Mycroft, wears a dark black cloak with a red edge on the collar. Once you get on the train, you can get to Victoria Station in time to take the express train to the European continent.

Watson did as required and got to the railway station smoothly. It was only seven minutes since he left the bus. Watson was looking for Holmes among a group of passengers and the farewell crowd, but there was no trace. I only saw an old Italian priest, speaking poor English, trying to make the porter understand that his luggage was to be checked into Paris. The siren sounded, and Holmes said hello to Watson. It turned out that the faltering Italian priest was Holmes.

After the train started, a tall man appeared in the crowd, waving his hand constantly, as if he wanted to stop the train. This person was probably (presumably) a pawn sent by Mauriati. This confirms the basis for Holmes to believe that the intuitive field exists.

They said they were going to France, but they got off at Canterbury Station halfway and then transferred to other countries in Europe.However, whether in a simple and remote Alpine village or in a sparsely populated mountain pass, Holmes always mobilized his keen and outstanding observation - intuitive ability. He quickly cast a wary eye on everyone passing by them, carefully looked at them, and tried to identify the traitors. After a long time of intense observation and thought, there appeared a "hard wound" of intuition—nervousness.

They passed through Jimmy Hill Pass and walked along the border of the Dawbenny Mountains. Suddenly, a big rock fell from the right ridge and rolled into the lake behind them. Holmes immediately ran up the ridge, stood on the top of the high peak, and looked around. Although the guide assured him that it was a common phenomenon for rocks to fall here in spring, he still could not dispel his doubts (doubtful type).Holmes was silent, but he smiled at Watson with an expression that seemed to have expected it.

For another example, in "The Adventures of the Empty House," Holmes placed a wax figure of himself in his room, asked Mrs. Harrison to kneel on the floor, moved her position every quarter of an hour, and created a scene of Holmes working under the weak light through the curtains, which was really duped by his followers.

Sherlock Holmes's counter intuitive field entered the field of concealment when he came to The Adventures of the Empty House:

In the short time before Moriarty fell into the waterfall and sank to the bottom of the pool, Holmes' brain ran at a high speed and quickly grasped a decision. First, he pretended to die and let the hidden Moriarty's minions show up, then appeared again, and finally waited for an opportunity to kill them. Therefore, instead of leaving their footprints in the Grand Canyon, even the reverse ones, they chose the risky rock climbing to escape, and then disappeared for three years. In addition to his brother's knowledge, even his "best friend" Watson was kept in the dark. The concealment of this scene is flawless.

Field concealment is the opposite of field leakage. Concealment in the field refers to the conscious "stealth" behavior taken against the enemy. It covers up and hides the details that may expose identity, whereabouts, motivation, purpose, etc. in a reasonable and impeccable form. Concealment can be either a detective or a criminal in the crime department.

"The Five Orange Pips" reflects the criminals' painstaking and impeccable concealment:The person concerned, John Opponshaw's uncle, opened a letter on March 10. There were three "K" characters scribbled in red ink on the inner layer of the envelope cover. Five dried orange rips fell from the envelope. He was scared out of his wits.From then on, he behaved abnormally, drank heavily all day long, became crazy after drinking, and his heart was filled with fear.On the night of May 2, seven weeks later, he was drunk again and suddenly ran out.He was found lying in a cesspool in the garden. No signs of violence were found, and the water in the pit was only two feet deep. In view of his usual eccentric behavior, the police concluded that this was a suicide. But he was a man afraid of death, and he didn't believe that he would run out to seek his own views. Father inherited his estate and savings.

On the the fourth day after New Year's Day, when everyone was having breakfast, my father suddenly screamed, and five dried orange stones fell from the envelope that had just been opened. He used to laugh at the absurdity of his uncle's experience, but now he was also scared and lost in a trance.

On the third day, my father went to visit his old friends to relax. The next day, I received a telegram from his friend saying that his father had an accident.He fell into a deep lime pit and was unconscious. There was no sign of violence, no footprints, no robbery, and no record of passers-by. Therefore, the coroner made the conclusion of "accidental death"." And yet I need not tell you that my mind was far from at ease, and that I was well-nigh certain that some foul plot had been woven round him."

John Opponshaw inherited the inheritance under such an ominous circumstance. Two years and eight months later, one morning, the disaster came again. The situation was the same as that of my uncle and father. Five small, dry orange stones were poured out of an envelope. The envelope also contains: "K.K.K.!"

"To tell the truth, I have felt helpless. I have felt like one of those poor rabbits when the snake is writhing towards it. I seem to be in the grasp of some resistless, inexorable evil, which no foresight and no precautions can guard against."

John Opponshaw called the police."But they listened to my story with a smile. I am convinced that the inspector has formed the opinion that the letters are all practical jokes, and that the deaths of my relations were really accidents, as the jury stated, and were not to be connected with the warnings."

One night a few days later, someone suddenly fell into the water and called for help. It was very dark at that time, and the storm was raging. After the assistance of the police and the people, a body was finally retrieved. The body was identified as John Opponshaw. The body showed no signs of violence. It was also believed that the deceased was killed by accident.

This hideout was finally exposed by Holmes—it was the work of the huge and infamous Ku Klux Klan in the United States.

Field leakage means that your thoughts, thoughts and actions are inadvertently disclosed in your words and deeds and are detected by the other party. This is caused by improper concealment. The consequences of field leakage on the investigation field are serious, ranging from missed opportunities to fish and trees. If it is an act of deliberately revealing, creating confusion and deceiving the other party, it belongs to an anti intuition field.

THE RETURN OF SHERLOCK HOLMES

1. The Adventure of the Empty House

A. Holmes and Watson Have Different Observations

WATSON ACCOMPANIED HOLMES TO OBSERVE THE WATCHERS IN THE SHELTER. THE STREETS WERE crowded with pedestrians. It was a cold and noisy night. Most people were wrapped in coats and scarves, which brought great difficulties to the observers. Once or twice, Watson seemed to see similar people he had just seen, especially two people who seemed to be sheltering from the wind in a nearby doorway, so he asked Holmes to pay attention to them, but he "gave a little ejaculation of impatience", said no, and continued to look at the street without turning his eyes.

For mountains, different people observe different results. Observation, like intuition, is closely related to one's career, education background, experience and even temperament type.Due to the above differences, the perspective and tendency of observation and intuition are also selected. This is the truth that "everyone loves each flower, and each flower goes to each eye".Of course, from another perspective, the intensity and depth of observation vary from person to person.Compared with Holmes, Watson's observation ability is naturally limited.Watson also recognized this, but it would be unfair if Watson attributed Holmes' extraordinary observation to his "superhuman senses".In fact, Watson knew that Holmes' training of observation was close to "devil training". This may be one of the things Watson needs to work hard on.

B. Holmes and Watson's Outlook on Looks

Most of the descriptions or narrations about looks in the works are done by Watson, while Holmes is rare. In "The Final Problem," Holmes expressed to Mauritia, the leader of the criminal group, as follows:

He is very tall, thin, with a raised forehead, deep eyes, a shaven face, and a pale face. He is a bit like an ascetic monk and has the demeanor of a professor. He stooped and stretched his face forward, looking strange and vulgar. These statements should be said to be neutral, without comment, praise or derogation. Through his appearance, we didn't see that he had any special disposition. It seems that Holmes is not interested in physiognomy or osteography or has some reservations.

Watson is different. His description of many characters is obviously tendentious and controversial. Look at his description of Mauriati's minion, Colonel Moran:

He was an elderly man, with a small protruding nose, a high forehead and a large gray beard; his face was thin and dark, energetic and treacherous, full of fierce wrinkles;he has a philosopher's forehead and a lascivious man's chin;he has drooping eyelids, cold blue eyes, fierce nose and aggressive eyebrows.Everyone can recognize that this is the most obvious danger signal of that person.The fierce old man kept silent and stared at my partner; his wild eyes and upturned beard looked like a tiger.

Appearance is the inherent material basis that is difficult to change. What is presented to people is the skin and flesh that has little change, even seems to remain unchanged. Are there any secrets that people can know hidden in their skin or bones? Or can appearance reveal a person's character, even criminal potential or prosperity?

Italian criminologist Roberto Roebrosau has a theory of congenital crime. He classifies human heads from their physiological characteristics. People with this type of characteristics are easy to commit this kind of crime, while people with that type of characteristics are easy to commit that kind of crime. This theory seems to have some practical basis, but it also has obvious limitations and one-sided, mainly because the experimental objects are basically prisoners in custody. Nevertheless, it still has a great influence on later generations.

According to his theory, the police authorities have printed and distributed a police manual on people's faces for reference by patrols and investigators.

Characteristics of violent appearance: flat forehead, flat back, short and horizontal head, large protruding or concave eyes, sharp vision of upper vision, large horizontal nose, exposed cheeks, protruding ears, and ear tips. Types liable to commit crimes: arson, assault, homicide, injury, robber, intimidation, infringement, escape.

Greed features: big face, hooked nose, big mouth, thick lips, big chin, short head. Types easy to commit crimes: theft, embezzlement, fraud, gambling, stolen goods.

Vanity features: round forehead, big eyes, flowing vision, weak and drooping eyebrows, many mustaches, large lower lip, tip of nose and big ears. The types that are easy to commit crimes: adultery, abortion, abandonment, and crimes against marriage and family decency.

Intrinsic features: long face, low and flat forehead, small eyes, short nose, oblique mouth, tooth tip, ear process.Types liable to commit crimes: forgery, false accusation, fraud, breach of trust, concealment, and obstruction of order.

Idleness features: small forehead, large chin, thick eyebrows, loose nose, and small eyes. Types easy to commit crimes: opium, stolen goods, floating waves.

It is impossible to verify whether or not this gentleman's theory has practical guiding significance in policing practice, and how much guiding significance it has.It should be considered that appearance implies rather than reveals certain personality traits, which seems to be better understood and easier to accept.People will show a temperament or aura in a specific environment and mood.Through this temperament and aura, intuition can roughly grasp certain personality characteristics of the person concerned, as well as "good face", "bad face", "good heart", "bad heart", or both. Then, through constant exploration and investigation, we can find evidence to verify, or use logical reasoning to demonstrate.Many detectives have this "skill", which is just the accumulation of their long-term life and case work, but it is also impossible to see whether a person has committed a certain crime or any trace of having committed a crime from the person's appearance.

Good looks can delight people's mood. A good mood can't help but respond to requests; good looks often cover all the ugly. Seeing trees instead of forests makes people lose their senses and make judgments unbalanced.

Zeng Guofan, a famous minister in modern times, attached great importance to appearance when promoting and appointing cadres, and he also wrote books. He was a master of integrating theory with practice in this field.In his famous book "Accurately Identify People," "the way to know people" pays attention to taste and affection, which is commendable; however, the "method of meeting people" is biased and arbitrary.

Zeng Guofan believed that people with beautiful eyes that grow to the hair must hold the judicial power; those who have balding but connect with the denomination can hold the power of money and grain.He even believed that: whether a person is evil or positive, you can tell by his eyes and nose; whether he is true or not, you can tell by looking at his lips; whether he can establish fame depends on his mettle; whether he can be rich or not depends on his spirit; If he has an idea, you can tell by his fingers; whether he will have a storm, you can tell by his hamstring; If you want to see whether he is organized, it is all in his speeches.Zeng Guofan found the physiological basis for people's essence, spirit, splendor, wealth and even life, old age, illness and death from their appearance, which was too metaphysical.In real life, there are countless people whose looks are inversely proportional to their hearts; In the practice of investigation, the cases of appearance misleading investigation and misleading the victim also occur from time to time.For example, Joseph, who gives the image of a straightforward, sunny, innocent and naughty boy in "The Naval Treaty," is a gangster who steals state secret documents for personal gain regardless of the future or even life of his brother-in-law to be. His image has confused the promising diplomat's brother-in-law to be Percy and others.

Man is the most complex creature, and many physiological and psychological phenomena of man still need to be understood; the world people live in is also unpredictable, and more natural phenomena need to be explored. We can see people's spirit and spirit from their appearance, and we can believe it; but If you want to see the future and destiny of people from their appearance, you can only make fun of them.

I believe many people fresh memories of Zhang Yingying's case. In April 2017, Zhang Yingying went to the University of Illinois in the United States for exchange and study. Unfortunately, the tragedy happened on June 9. After class at noon, she returned to the apartment for dinner as usual.At about 1:39 p.m., she received the renewal information from the rent administrator, and the two decided to meet at 2:10 p.m.While waiting for the bus, Zhang Yingying was watched by Chris Tengsen and got on his car. Since she did not return until 9:00 p.m., the police launched an investigation after receiving the alarm. After more than two years of investigation, Chris Tensen finally admitted the fact of killing Zhang Yingying.

A celebrity once posted a blog post: [Zhang Yingying has a high probability of survival]During the lunch break, I called Master Liu and asked him to analyze her face in addition to Zhang Yingying's eight characters. Master Liu said: She has a full sky, a round ground pavilion, a straight nose and big ears. She is not short-lived, but the sky is too high, which is easy to cause emotional wind. He suggested that the police solve the case from the perspective of emotional turmoil.Whether the master's opinion is correct or not will not be explored here.

In the next "The Norwood Builder,", when all the unfavorable evidence points to Holmes' client MacFarlane, Watson also sweats for him and hopes that "the man's appearance would go far with any jury". Holmes immediately pointed out: "That is a dangerous argument, my dear Watson. You remember that terrible murderer, Bert Stevens, who wanted us to get him off in '87? Was there ever a more mild-mannered, Sunday-school young man?" Watson agrees with this view.

Holmes does not praise or disparage the appearance of the suspect, does not make comments, does not judge people by their appearance, does not give priority to preconceptions, is objective and calm, and speaks with evidence, which fully demonstrates the rationality and fair and just professional ethics of a big detective.

2. The Norwood Builder

A. Holmes' Intuition Show (No. 21):

A young man, pale and disheveled, rushed into the house like a maniac. He was Holmes' client, MacFarlane. After apologizing for his recklessness, he introduced himself. Holmes said you were a bachelor, a lawyer, a freemason and an asthmatic.

The young man was stunned:Yes, you are talking about me.

Sherlock Holmes didn't need to explain this time, but Watson also learned to reason and speculate because he was influenced by Holmes:

Bachelor} slovenly, about twenty years old;

Lawyer} carries a pile of documents with him, and the certificate is exposed in the pocket of his coat

Mason} amulet on his watch chain

Asthmatic} his wheezing voice

B. Holmes and Sheriff Lestrade's Intuitive Comparison

In the face of the murder case of the architect Odek, Holmes grasped the most important clue of the case—the will from the very beginning. He found the will very strange(doubtful type). Why? Because he saw something unusual from the draft of the will.Why?

It can be seen that the first few lines and the middle sentences on the second page, as well as the last one or two lines, are as clear as they were printed. Everything else was not written clearly. There are three places that can't be recognized at all. It is speculated that it was written on the train:

The clear part should be that the train stops at the station, the unclear part should be that the train is running, and the least clear part is that the train is passing the turnout. This is written on a suburban railway line, because only in the vicinity of a big city can one meet the turnout one after another.

Further doubt: It's strange that such an important document should be written in such a casual way.

Further speculation: it indicates that he did not actually attach importance to this will, or did not intend to make it effective at all.

Lieutenant General Lestrade believed that the will had nothing to do with the case. He only valued the evidence and witnesses on the spot. It was this young man MacFarlane who did it. He also believed that the will was the cause of architect Odek's self inflicted misfortune."Well, he drew up his own death warrant at the same time," said Lestrade. In order to show the correctness of his views, he speculated on McFarlane's criminal motives:

"Here is a young man who learns suddenly that, if a certain older man dies, he will succeed to a fortune. What does he do? He says nothing to anyone, but he arranges that he shall go out on some pretext to see his client that night.He waits until the only other person in the house is in bed, and then in the solitude of a man's room he murders him, burns his body in the wood-pile, and departs to a neighbouring hotel. The blood-stains in the room and also on the stick are very slight. It is probable that he imagined his crime to be a bloodless one, and hoped that if the body were consumed it would hide all traces of the method of his death–traces which, for some reason, must have pointed to him. Is not all this obvious?"

But Holmes thought it was too simple and obvious. It was completely from phenomenon to phenomenon, completely at the level of directness. So Holmes put forward four questions (doubtful type):

1. Put it in perspective, will you choose the night when you made your will to commit murder?
2. Is it not dangerous for you to keep your will and murder so close together in time?
3. Would you choose the servant to open the door and let you in to leave a witness?
4. Will you destroy the body and leave a cane to show that you are the murderer?

Lestrade believed that the walking stick was left by the criminal in a panic. At the same time, I hope Holmes can give him a conjecture that conforms to the facts.

Although Holmes gave some of his own speculations, Lestrade was not convinced, because from the current evidence, Lestrade had the upper hand.At this time, Holmes was in a very contradictory and embarrassing situation. He said to Watson, "All my instincts are one way, and all the facts are the other..." Intuition points to the innocence of the client MacFarlane, which is Holmes' point of view.The facts point that MacFarlane's evidence is conclusive and his responsibility cannot escape. This is Lestrade's view. Follow his intuition, or follow the current "facts" and "evidence"? Holmes still believed his intuition, continued to investigate and found evidence for his intuition.

The housekeeper should be an insider, but she can't ask. "There was a sort of sulky defiance in her eyes, which only goes with guilty knowledge." Holmes saw the problem from the housekeeper's eyes, and was helpless.

When Lestrede told Holmes that he had obtained new important evidence fingerprint and advised him to give up the investigation of the case, Holmes said very calmly: "After all, important fresh evidence is a two-edged thing, and may possibly cut in a very different direction to that which Lestrade imagines." This shows that Holmes' intuitive thinking level has reached the dialectical level of pure emotion. Indeed, it was this so-called new important evidence that made the whole case unexpectedly reverse.So Holmes speculated on the source of this new important evidence according to the existing clues:

That night, when they sealed the packet of letters with enamel, Odec asked MacFarlane to firmly press the hot enamel on one of the envelopes with his thumb.The young man will naturally do this, and I believe that even he has forgotten about it.Odek himself didn't want to use it at that time. Later, when he was thinking about the case in the secret room, he thought that he could use the fingerprint to make hard evidence of MacFarlane's guilt. Just take a wax mold on the enamel print, apply it to the mold with needle bleeding, and then press it on the wall in person or ask the housekeeper at night.Holmes finally affirmed that the documents he brought into the secret room should be checked, and the paint print with fingerprints must be found. I can bet.

Lestrade agreed with this.

In addition, Holmes found that a large amount of money had been transferred to a Mr. Cornelias when he looked through the bank passbook. Holmes made an accurate guess:

I guess Cornelius is himself, using another name. I believe these cheques were all deposited in the bank of a small town in another place under that name. Odek often went to that town to live a dual identity life. He plans to change his name in the future, take out the money, and then go somewhere else to start all over again.

Lestrade fully agreed.

3. The Dancing Men

福尔摩斯的直觉秀（No .22）：

Holmes' Intuition Show (No. 22):

"So, Watson," said Holmes, suddenly, "you do not propose to invest in South African securities?" Watson was shocked. Although Watson knew Sherlock Holmes' various strange skills, he could not explain what was on his mind with such a statement.

"How on earth do you know that?" Watson asked.Holmes said his reasoning and speculation:

华生不打算
在南非投资了} 左手的虎口

1、昨晚你从俱乐部回来，你左手虎口上有白粉；
2、打台球时为了稳定球杆才在虎口上抹白粉；
3、没有瑟斯顿做伴，你从不打台球。
4、此外，你四周说过，瑟斯顿有购买某项南非产业的特权，再有一个月就到期了，他很想叫你跟他共同使用；
5、你的支票簿锁在我的抽屉里，你一直没跟我要过钥匙。

1. Last night when you came back from the club, you had white powder on your left tiger's mouth;
2. When playing billiards, white powder is applied to the tiger's mouth in order to stabilize the club;
    Watson doesn't plan to
3. Invested in South Africa} Tiger Mouth on the Left Hand3. Without Thurston as a companion, you never played billiards.
4. In addition, you have said around that Thurston has the privilege to purchase a certain South African industry, which will expire in another month. He would very much like you to share it with him;
5. Your checkbook is locked in my drawer, and you haven't been with me I asked for the key.

4. The Solitary Cyclist

Holmes' Intuition Show (No. 23):

Miss Smith, a beautiful uninvited guest, went into Holmes' Residence on Baker Street and asked for help. Holmes looked at her with his burning eyes and said, "...so ardent a bicyclist must be full of energy."

She glanced down in surprise at her own feet, and I observed the slight roughening of the side of the sole caused by the friction of the edge of the pedal."Yes, I bicycle a good deal, Mr. Holmes, and that has something to do with my visit to you to-day."

Holmes took the lady's ungloved hand, and examined it with as close an attention and as little sentiment as a scientist would show to a specimen. "You will excuse me, I am sure. It is my business," said he, as he dropped it. "I nearly fell into the error of supposing that you were typewriting. Of course, it is obvious that it is music."

Holmes said, the spatulate finger-ends is common to both professions. Why do musicians have the same hands as typists? Holmes did not explain this, but this is introduced later in the work. "We are thrown rather together. I play his accompaniments in the evening." The accompaniment must be the use of musical instruments. Judging from the hand type described by Holmes, it is probably due to the frequent use of keyboard instruments—pianos.

In "The Sign of Four," Holmes once introduced a small paper that he thought was novel, which explained the influence of occupation on human hands, and attached the hand type insertions of stone tile workers, sailors, woodcarvers, typesetters, weavers and diamond grinders. He believed that these were of great practical value for scientific investigation, especially in identifying unknown corpses and understanding the identity of criminals.

"There is a spirituality about the face, however, which the typewriter does not generate. This lady is a musician." Holmes found out the difference between typists and musicians by intuiting the temperament of beautiful women.

"Yes, Mr. Holmes, I teach music." The beauty confirms this statement.

Holmes continued to speculate: "In the country, I presume, from your complexion."

What kind of face can reflect the difference between urban and rural areas? Holmes did not introduce. It is likely that there are more opportunities to work in the countryside, and the skin is relatively dark. I can only speculate.

"Yes, sir, near Farnham, on the borders of Surrey." The beauty once again confirmed Holmes' conjecture.

5. The Priory Schools(Not discussed)

6. Black Peter

Holmes' Intuitive Investigation:

A mysterious case happened in Woodman Lee Manor. Peter Gary, the old captain who was hated by his neighbors and even his wife and daughter, was stabbed to death in his cabin, which was called "small cabin".Sheriff Hopkins and Holmes found that the door lock had been pried and the door had not been opened when they were inspecting the scene in the cabin. It looked like a novice thief.So they decided to stay in the pit and wait for the current situation. At 2:30 in the middle of the night, they really caught a weak young man, pale and over twenty, who tried to enter the cabin again.Sheriff Hopkins was elated at the case. Holmes thought the case was not over yet. Hopkins speculated about the case based on the evidence he had:

It was found that Nairgan stayed in the Brandblatt Hotel on the day of the crime and pretended to play golf.His room was on the first floor, which was convenient for access. That night, when he went to Woodmanley to meet the old captain Peter Gary in the cabin, they quarreled. Nalgen stabbed the old captain to death with a harpoon.He lost his notebook when he ran out in fear. He wanted to ask the captain about various securities. You may have noticed the marks marked on the securities, which were found and traced in the London market, and others may still be in the hands of Captain Gary.According to Nairgan's confession, he was eager to take back the securities belonging to his father in order to repay the creditors.After he ran away, he was afraid of the cabin, but in order to get the information he needed, he had to go to the cabin again. The case is very obvious and clear!

Holmes smiled, shook his head, and put forward a different point of view from the police chief: He can't kill anyone at all. (Concluding type) Then he raised three questions (doubtful type):

Can this young man, who has no power to bind the chicken, throw a steel fork through his chest and insert it into the wall?

Was it he and Black Peter who drank rum at midnight?

Was it his profile that the mason saw on the curtain of the hut two days ago?

Holmes further speculated: No, no... it must be a strong and powerful person. We must find this person.

Holmes denied Sheriff Hopkins's intuitive speculation, informed him of the correct direction of investigation, and successfully captured the real murderer—Patrick Cairns, a seaman harpoon.

From the very beginning, Holmes grasped the accurate clues, and the excellent facts: amazing strength, the skills of using harpoons, rum, seal skin tobacco bags, which remind people of a seaman and a whale hunter.He was sure that the initials "P.C." on the tobacco bag was a coincidence, not Peter Gary. He rarely smoked, and no pipe was found in the cabin. "You remember that I asked whether whisky and brandy were in the cabin. You said they were. How many landsmen are there who would drink rum when they could get these other spirits? Yes, I was certain it was a seaman."

7. Charles Augustus Milverton(Not discussed)

8. The Six Napoleons

The Main Process of Holmes' Intuitive Investigation:

Sheriff Lestrade told Holmes a very small but strange thing (suspicious type, the same below): "You wouldn't think there was anyone living at this time of day who had such a hatred of Napoleon the First that he would break any image of him that he could see." He thought it was madness.

The first one happened in Mos Hudson's shop. As soon as the clerk left the counter, he heard something striking each other. He immediately ran to the front of the shop and found a statue of Napoleon on the counter with other works of art had been smashed. He rushed to the street and did not find or recognize the man. He reported the matter to the policeman. The plaster statue is worth a few shillings at most, and the matter is too small to be investigated.

The second occurred in Dr. Barniko's home and clinic. Dr. Barniko admired Napoleon very much. He bought two plaster busts of Napoleon from Hudson's shop, one in the lobby of the Kenington Street residence and the other on the mantelpiece of the Lower Brexton Street clinic. In the morning, Dr. Barniko found that someone had broken into his house at night, without taking anything else, and only took the plaster head to the wall of the outside garden and smashed it into pieces. When he arrived at the clinic at twelve o'clock, he found that the window had been opened and the room was full of fragments of another Napoleon bust.

The three destroyed plasters are identical. Watson thought it was "paranoia". Holmes was skeptical of the views of Lester Reed and Watson (dubious type, the same below), because he could not explain that a crazy person or paranoid patient would find out the distribution of these plaster figures. In addition, there is a characteristic in this person's eccentric (abnormal) behavior: taking the plaster statue in Dr. Barniko's hall outside to smash it; In the clinic, he broke it when nobody was there.

From Holmes' experience, these seemingly insignificant details cannot be easily ignored. There must be (conclusive) deep-seated reasons.

The third time happened in the home of Mr. Horace Hack of the Central News Corporation. Not only did he take away Napoleon's plaster bust, but also there was a murder. There is a photograph of the deceased's remains. The person in the photo looks smart, with thick eyebrows and prominent nose and mouth, like the face of a baboon.

Holmes looked at the picture and asked how was the plaster statue? Sheriff Lestrade said that he had found it in the garden of an empty house in Camden Street, two or three hundred yards away from Huck's house, and it had been smashed to pieces. Small pieces of debris were scattered on the grass. Holmes picked up several pieces of debris and examined them carefully. Watson was convinced (conclusive) that he had made new discoveries by observing Holmes' attentive face and manner.

Holmes said that he had mastered some facts that could be used as a basis for action. From the perspective of the perpetrator, first, the plaster statue was much more valuable than human life; second, the bust was only for breaking, and it was not broken in or near the house; third, it is broken at street lamps or places with lights. Holmes said:This is also a strange thing.(Doubt type, the same below.)

Holmes asked Lestrade to tell Mr. Huck that when he wrote the report, he said that there was a pervert murderer who hated Napoleon in his family. This is the anti intuition field where Holmes plays hard to get and disturbs the audience. Obviously, Lestrade did not understand. He was puzzled (the same below), stared at him and said, "You don't seriously believe that?"

Holmes said: "It is possible that I may have to ask your company and assistance upon a small expedition which will have to be undertaken to-night, if my chain of reasoning should prove to be correct. Until then good-bye and good luck!" It shows that he has a new idea on the case (speculative type).

Then Holmes and Watson went to investigate the context of the plaster statue. Holmes said, "I am, as you have no doubt surmised, endeavouring to trace these busts to their source, in order to find if there is not something peculiar which may account for their remarkable fate.Watson, you must have guessed (speculative type, the same below).

They found out that there was an Italian named Bei Bo in the two cases of Kenington Street and Kensington. The appearance of this person indicates the correct direction of case investigation.

Sheriff Lestrade had a guess about the case:

Detective Hill recognized Huck when he saw the body killed at his house.His name was Pietro Vanuzzi. He came from Naples and was a famous robber in London. He had connections with the mafia.The Mafia is a secret political organization, which wants to realize its creed through assassination.Now it seems that things are getting clearer.The other person (referring to the murderer) may also be an Italian and a mafia.He probably violated some aspect of Mafia discipline. Pietro was following him. The picture in Pietro's pocket may be the man. He followed the man and saw him enter a house. He waited outside. Later, he was fatally injured in the scuffle.

Holmes agreed with the sheriff's speculation, but wondered why he had no explanation for the plaster statue.Lestrade also felt strange and said: Plaster statue! You can never forget the plaster statue. That's nothing.It's just a small theft. He can be locked up for six months at most.We're investigating murder. The next step is to find someone according to the photos and arrest him for murder.

Their investigation directions diverged, and Holmes planned to find another way to achieve his goal more easily.However, Holmes felt:It seems uncertain about this. It all depends —it depends on a factor that we can't control at all. But there is great hope— we can say that we are two thirds sure.Sometimes the goal of intuition is obscure and inexplicable, but it is often very reliable and accurate, just like a huge force that deeply attracts our thinking to move forward, and we will never stop until we reach the goal.

Holmes wanted to look for the murderer in Chizwick District, because the investigation found that the only two plaster buildings were located at Mr. Josiah Brown's house in Labnum Street in Chizwick District and Mr. Sandford's house in Lower Jungle Street in Reading District.Holmes speculated that the killer would prefer to commit the crime in the nearby Chizwick District of London. Therefore, he first asked the correspondent to send an urgent letter to Brown and take precautions.Then he went up to the attic and looked through the bound copies of old newspapers.It took him a long time to come downstairs with a satisfied look in his eyes. This was Watson's observation. Watson guessed that he found information in the newspaper that would help solve the case and confirm his investigation ideas. At the same time, Watson also guessed that the purpose of going to Chizwick was to catch the murderer on the spot.

Watson appreciated Holmes' counterintuitive measures and asked Huck to write in the newspaper that the murderer was mentally disordered rather than deliberately murdered, making the murderer think he can continue to commit crimes with impunity.

The murderer continued to commit the crime. They finally caught the murderer —Beibo, who looked like a baboon's face in the photos of the deceased's remains, near Brown in Chizwick District.

However, what puzzled Watson and others (dubious type) was that Holmes did not pay attention to the person he caught, but squatted on the steps to carefully inspect the plaster statue that had been broken into small pieces.Holmes took the fragments to the light and carefully examined them. It seemed that there was something special about these gypsum fragments. In fact, Holmes' investigative thinking had shifted to the fragments of the gypsum statue. He speculated that what he found in the fragments of the gypsum statue should be the purpose of double wave, and killing was an accessory product.

At this time, Sheriff Lestrade reported the results of the interrogation of Beibo. He refused to answer the reasons for the destruction of these plaster statues. The police estimated that he might have made the statues himself.

On the surface, Holmes seemed to listen to the sheriff's words politely. In fact, he was absent-minded. His thoughts had wandered elsewhere. Under his usual facial expressions, he was mixed with anxiety and expectation. At last, he stood up from his chair, his eyes shining —this was Watson's observation of Holmes' inner activities.

Watson guessed right. At this moment, Holmes is thinking whether Mr. Sandford of Reading District will come as promised. If this gentleman breaks his promise, he will not only make a fool of himself in front of Lester Reed and Watson, but also affect his ten pound bet and whether he will reveal the truth of the case.

Mr. Sandford arrived as promised. Holmes bought the plaster statue for only 15 shillings for 10 pounds and signed the relevant agreement. These behaviors aroused everyone's doubts.

Then Holmes took out a piece of white cloth from the drawer, spread it on the table, and put the newly bought plaster statue of Napoleon in the middle of the white cloth. He took up his shotgun and put a shot on the top of Napoleon's statue, and the plaster statue immediately turned into pieces. Holmes anxiously examined the fragments. After a while, he held up a piece of debris with something like a raisin on a pudding and shouted.

Gentlemen, let me introduce the famous Black Pearl of Baugus to you!—Holmes' conjecture was confirmed.

Lestrade and Watson were stunned. Then Holmes uncovered the case.

This pearl was the priceless treasure lost by the prince of Cologne in the bedroom of the Dakor Hotel. At that time, the police in London were futile. They also asked Holmes, and he could do nothing. However, he suspected the princess's maid. She was an Italian, and the authorities found out that she had a brother in London. He thought(speculation type)that Pietro, who was killed two days ago, was her brother. He also checked the date in the newspaper. The pearl was lost two days before Beibo was arrested. The reason for the arrest of Beibo was that he was arrested in Gelder Company for injuring others. At that time, Beibo was making a statue. Beibo gets the pearl. It may be stolen from Pietro, or it may be Pietro's accomplice, or it may be the intermediary between Pietro and his sister. But it doesn't matter. The important fact is that he has the pearl. Within a few minutes of the police's arrest, Beibo had a brainwave and stuffed the pearl into the partially dried plaster statue. After he was released from prison, with the help of his cousins and other Italian employees working for Gelder Company, he found the whereabouts of the plaster statue that had been sold and might have hidden pearls, and tried to retrieve the pearls. As a result, a series of strange cases occurred.

9. The Three Students

Mr. Sommertz's Doubts:

Mr. Hilton Somtz, the tutor of St. Luke's College, found that the examination sample put in his study had been secretly read and copied.Holmes is invited to participate in the investigation to recover the influence because of the high scholarship. The case involved three students and servants of Mr. Sommertz. They live in the same building.

The person living below is Jill Crist, an excellent student and an excellent player. He has participated in the college football team and cricket team. He has won awards in low hurdles and long jump. He is a handsome and elegant boy. Father lost his fortune because of horse racing. His family is very poor, but he is hardworking with a promising future.

In the middle is Indian humanitarian Rath Reis. He is a quiet but inaccessible person, as most Indians are. He studies very well, but his Greek is worse. He is steady and methodical.

Miles McClaren lives above, and he is the most talented one in this university. However, he is capricious and dissolute, and he was almost expelled for playing cards. I have been loafing around this semester and must be very afraid of this scholarship exam.

Servant Bannister was in his fifties. He had followed Mr. Sommertz for many years and was an honest man.

Mr. Somtz suspected(suspicious type, the same below)Bannister at first, but he sincerely denied it and believed that he was telling the truth. Then he suspected that Jill Christie, who lived below, did it. "But, of the three, he is perhaps the least unlikely." Finally, I suspect that McClaren lives above, because when they investigate these students one by one, they not only do not open the door but also hear angry insults from the door. Mr. Somtz blushed with anger and said, "How rude! Even if he didn't know it was me who knocked, wouldn't it be rude to do so? In this case, he is very suspicious."

Indian student Dorat Reis is also questionable.First, he is the only person who has been to Mr. Sommertz's study after receiving the test paper; second, he is silent, short, with a crooked nose; third, I saw him in the room downstairs as if he was fidgeting around. When he went to his room to investigate, he "looked at us askance". When Holmes finished drawing the architectural structure and was ready to leave, he looked very relaxed and happy.

Watson's opinion: The guy who lives above has the worst character. That Indian is also very cunning. The servant "impressed me as a very honest man."

Holmes' opinion:For McClaren above, every moment is precious when you are preparing to take the exam the next day, when a group of people suddenly come to you, you will treat them like this. That doesn't mean anything. Indians seem to be restless, because some people often walk around when they try to remember things. When Holmes heard that the servant had left the key on the door, he thought, "Isn't it very unusual (suspicious type) for you to do this when the test paper is in the room?"

The phenomenon is complicated and confusing, and there are different opinions. Who is the real perpetrator? According to Holmes' investigation, it was the polite "promising" Gilchrist who lived below, while the seemingly "honest" servant Bannister was the patron, which was quite different from people's immediate impression. The result of this error is that people's perception is superficial and does not go deep into the root.

Mr. Somtz's perception of the suspect is always at the level of directness. In the face of the complex phenomena before him, he suspects Bannister, Jill Christie, and finally McLaren. In this way of catching wind and catching shadows, the doubt built on the basis of no stone hammer evidence is just a wild guess. Watson was also confused by the superficial phenomenon of these people. Only Sherlock Holmes kept his composure and reason from beginning to end. With his keen observation ability, he kept his hot eyed thinking at the level of intuition, even reached the level of perfect dialectics, so as to ensure the impartial direction of investigation and driving in the right channel.

10. The Golden Pince-Nez

Holmes' Intuition Show (No. 24):

At the scene of the murder, the victim pulled off the murderer's gold rimmed pinnose glasses. Holmes carefully observed the glasses and put them on the bridge of his nose to test things. He went to the window to look out, and then went to the light to closely examine them. Finally, he wrote the psychological portrait of the victim—intuition show to Detective Hopkins.

Hopkins read: It's a lady who dresses decently and looks like an aristocrat. The nose is very wide, the eyes are close to the nose, there are wrinkles on the forehead, the face is dull and stereotyped, and maybe there is a little shoulder shaving. There are indications that she has been to the same optical shop at least twice in recent months. Her glasses are very strong. There are not many optical shops in this city, so it is not difficult to find her.

When Hopkins and Watson looked very surprised, Holmes smiled and made a retrospective inference:

Considering the delicacy of the glasses and the last words of the deceased, it is not difficult to infer that it is a lady;

She is an elegant and respectable person, because the person wearing gold rimmed glasses will not be sloppy in dress;

The clip of glasses is very wide, indicating that the bottom of a woman's nose is very wide. Such a nose is generally short and thick, but there are many exceptions, so I dare not be too arbitrary. My face is long and narrow, but my eyes are not aligned with the center of the lens, which shows that this lady's eyes are very close to her nose;

The lens is concave and deep in degree;

A person always squints to see things at ordinary times, which will inevitably have certain physiological effects, making forehead, eyelids and shoulders have certain characteristics.

These Watson expressed understanding, but he did not understand how to know that she had been to an optical shop twice?

Holmes made a further speculation:

As you can see, the clip of the glasses is lined with cork to prevent the nose from being sore. One piece of cork is faded and a little worn, while the other is new. It is obvious that a piece of cork has fallen and been replaced. And this old cork, I think, will only be installed for a few months. The two corks are identical, "so I gather that the lady went back to the same establishment for the second."

"By George, it's marvellous!" cried Hopkins,

11. The Abbey Grange

There was a murder in Grange Manor. The manor owner was killed and his wife was tied to a stool. Madame said that the killers were Randall and his two sons, who had committed crimes in West Denham, published in the newspaper two weeks ago.

A. Holmes' Intuition Show (No. 25):

In response to the murder at Grange Manor, Holmes said very definitely: "The crime was committed before twelve last night."

"How can you possibly tell?" asked Watson.

Holmes reasoned:

By an inspection of the trains, and by reckoning the time. The local police had to be called in, they had to communicate with Scotland Yard, Hopkins had to go out, and he in turn had to send for me. All that makes a fair night's work.

B. Two Strings of Doubts, One Insight to Reverse the Case

Holmes' doubts about the crime scene:

1. The knot tying the lady at the scene of the crime is very special;
2. He was interested in the purple bell rope that tied his wife;

    Holmes and Hopkins agreed that the murderer was familiar with the story and must have colluded with the servant. But Hopkins said the eight servants were well behaved. So, Holmes——
3. "It is necessary to suspect" the manor owner was angry with the maid who threw the water bottle at her, and "it will be suspicious" to the mistress.

Holmes' epiphany:

At this point, Holmes believed that the case was basically solved, as long as "it is not difficult to find out the accomplice after catching Randal." Although he and Watson were ready to return home, Holmes's face was still confused and confused.When they got on the train and were leaving, Holmes pulled Watson off the platform. "It's wrong –it's all wrong–I'll swear that it's wrong." Holmes suddenly had an epiphany. It was this epiphany that reversed the whole direction of investigation.

Holmes said:"Surely there are details in her story which, if we looked at in cold blood, would excite our suspicion." Then Holmes put forward six questions at one go (suspicious type):

1. The three Randals have been making a scene in West Denham two weeks ago. Their case and appearance have been published in the newspaper. Anyone who wants to make up a story about bandits will think of them;
2. It is usually not that early to commit a crime, nor will it stop a woman from shouting by hurting her. In fact, the more you hit her, the harder you will shout;
3. When the number of robbers is large enough to deal with one person, they generally do not kill;
4. Bandits are generally greedy. They will take whatever they can, not just a little;
5. The robbers usually drink all the wine and will not leave more than half of the bottle;
6. All three glasses are stained with wine, but only one has dross in it.

Holmes' doubts about the scene, his insight into the case, and his wife's doubts. The charm of doubt drove him to be "passionate" about the case, strip away the cocoon, and finally get out of the fog and reveal the bottom of the case. It turned out that this was a "bitter meat trick" in which the wife was protecting Captain Ekrock.

12. The Second Stain

Holmes' Intuitive Investigation:

One day, two famous European figures came to the humble apartment in Baker Street. They are Lord Bellinger, who has served as British Prime Minister twice, and Trony Hope, who is less than middle-aged, experienced and promising European Affairs Minister.They told Holmes that an important document had disappeared from Hope's home.Due to the political sensitivity of the document, it can not be investigated by the police department with too many people, but only by Holmes, a private detective with little information and good reputation.Mr. Hope introduced the missing documents.

Six days ago, we received a letter from a foreign monarch.This letter is so important that I dare not put it in the safe in my office, but take it to my home in Whitehall Residential Street every day and lock it in the file box in my bedroom.It was there last night, but it disappeared this morning.The file box stayed in my bedroom all night. My wife and I slept very little. I'm sure nobody came into the house at night. Neither my wife nor the housekeeping staff knew that this letter was stored at home.

After accepting the case, Holmes believed that only three intelligence dealers, Oberstein, LaLotier and Eduardo Lucas, had the courage to purchase and resell such important documents, and that Eduardo Lucas was the most likely one, because it only takes a few minutes to walk from Godolfen Street in Westminster Church District where he lives to Whitehall Residential Street where Hope lives.The possibility of establishing an explicit or implicit relationship between them (speculative type, the same below) is very high.Just as Holmes was about to find Lucas, he suddenly saw that the morning paper of the day published the news that Lucas had been assassinated at home.The important clues just sorted out were instantly destroyed.Meanwhile, Hope's beautiful wife came unexpectedly. She knew that she had lost important documents at home, so she wanted to know the contents of the important documents and judge the possible consequences for her husband. Holmes had no comment on this because he kept his promise of confidentiality. The lady had to go back sadly.

Although Holmes was fully committed, he often went back and forth to places such as Godolfen Street and Scotland Yard (London Police Station). After three days, there was no progress in the investigation.One day, Officer Lestrade asked Holmes to go to the scene to check a strange phenomenon.The blood stains on the carpet and on the ground are not symmetrical. That is to say, the carpet and the bloodstains on the ground were originally corresponding. It is likely that the carpet was moved after the body was removed.Lestrade said: "But what I want to know is, who shifted the carpet, and why?"

Holmes asked:"...has that constable in the passage been in charge of the place all the time?"

Lestrade said yes.Holmes said decisively:"Well, take my advice. Examine him carefully. Don't do it before us. We'll wait here. You take him into the back room. You'll be more likely to get a confession out of him alone. Ask him how he dared to admit people and leave them alone in this room. Don't ask him if he has done it.Take it for granted. Tell him you know someone has been here. Press him. Tell him that a full confession is his only chance of forgiveness. Do exactly what I tell you!"

At this time, Holmes had guessed that someone had trespassed on the scene, which must have a hidden purpose. Therefore, Lestrade was asked to question the gatekeeper in strict accordance with his requirements. At the same time, Holmes also speculated that there might be something famous under the carpet and wanted to check it in person.Then in the name of interrogating the gatekeeper, Lestrade was temporarily sent away from the scene. This is the witty Sherlock Holmes who killed two birds with one stone.

Holmes quickly opened the carpet and found a movable floor on the floor. After taking this floor away, he found a black hole. He reached in and found it empty.

Lestrade's interrogation also yielded results.As Holmes suspected, someone had entered the scene. The gatekeeper said that a beautiful lady had entered the scene out of "curiosity" and fainted at the scene after seeing the blood. When he went to buy brandy to save her, the lady left without saying goodbye.The constable said:"Well, sir, it was a bit rumpled, certainly, when I came back. You see, she fell on it and it lies on a polished floor with nothing to keep it in place. I straightened it out afterwards."

Before leaving, Holmes quietly took something out of his pocket and showed it to the guard. He stared at it intently and then exclaimed.Holmes put his forefinger on his lips, which meant that "the secrets of heaven must not be revealed".

Then Holmes and Watson went straight to Whitehall Residential Street. After painstaking efforts, they asked Mrs. Hope to take out the important document that she had taken away and taken back from under the Lucas' carpet, and put it back in Hope's file box intact, causing Hope to not really check the document.

However, the Prime Minister looked at Holmes and his eyes rolled. This is obviously doubted.

Holmes laughed away from his curious eyes. ""We also have our diplomatic secrets," said he as he picked up his hat and turned away.

Because Holmes had an accurate guess about the blood stains on the carpet at the scene of the crime, he locked the woman who had been to the scene out of curiosity as Mrs. Hope, and then uncovered the case that she was coerced by Lucas, an intelligence dealer, to steal this important document and exchange his wife's private letter before marriage. Lucas deserved to die at the hands of his insanity wife.

THE HOUNT OF THE BASKERVILLES

1. Mr. Sherlock Holmes

A. Holmes and Watson's Intuition Show (No. 26):

AT THE INSTIGATION OF HOLMES, HE AND WATSON HAD AN INTUITIVE SHOW ABOUT THE WALKING stick that Dr. Mortimer had left behind.

This is a walking stick, which is solemn, delicate, strong and practical, commonly used by old style private doctors. The wood of the cane is produced in Penang Island, and is called betelnut wood.There is a knot on the top, and below the top is a ring of wide silver hoop, which is about an inch wide. It is engraved with "To James Mortimer, a bachelor of the Royal College of Surgery, and friends of C.C.H.", and the time is "1884".

Watson:

1. Dr. Mortimer is an accomplished, older medical person who is highly respected.
2. He is probably a doctor who practises medicine in the countryside, and most of his visits are on foot. It's hard to imagine that a doctor who practices medicine in the city would still take it. The thick iron head installed at the lower end was also badly worn, and it was obvious that he had used it for many roads.
3. "And then again, there is the 'friends of the C.C.H.' I should guess that to be the Something Hunt, the local hunt to whose members he has possibly given some surgical assistance, and which has made him a small presentation in return."

105

Holmes:

1. It must be a doctor who practices medicine in the countryside, and he does often walk—— Holmes commented that Watson could not help saying:"Then I was right."
2. This gift for the doctor came from a hospital rather than a hunter's club, because the prefix "C.C." was placed before the word "hospital". It naturally reminds people of the words "Charing Cross";
3. Before going to the countryside, he once practiced medicine in the city. "I think that we might venture a little farther than this." The walking stick was sent by him when he was transferred from the urban hospital to the rural medical practice;
4. He may just be a resident surgeon or a resident physician;
5. From the date of his departure five years ago, which was engraved on the cane, he should be a young man under 30 years old;
6. He is affable, complacent and careless. According to my experience, those who treat others kindly will receive souvenirs; Only those who are not greedy for fame will give up their careers in London and go to the countryside; Only those who do things carelessly will stay in your room for an hour without leaving their business cards, but leave their walking sticks;
7. There is a pet dog, bigger than the average dog, smaller than the mastiff. Dogs often follow their masters with walking sticks in their mouths, and their teeth marks are clearly visible. From the gap between teeth marks, the jaw of a dog is wider than that of an ordinary dog, but narrower than that of a mastiff. It may be a curly haired long eared dog (actually, he has seen it with his own eyes from the window sill at this time, which is a joke).

Truth:

He is a typical village doctor. He is very untidy, his coat is dirty, and his trousers are worn.Although young, his back has been bent. With noble kindness. The walking stick was sent by Charing Cross Hospital as a wedding gift, but he left the hospital as soon as he got married. He is a graduate of the School of Surgery. He has a long eared dog with curly hair.

It can be seen from the above that under the influence of Sherlock Holmes, Watson's intuitive level has improved, but it is not enough. The accuracy rate needs to be further improved.Although Holmes was inaccurate in the apparent cause of the cane gift, the real reason was still acceptable. Moreover, even if two experts face the same thinking object, it is normal to have different opinions based on their different life and work experiences and knowledge structures.

2. The Curse of the Baskervilles

B. Holmes' Intuition Show (No. 27):

"I have in my pocket a manuscript," said Dr. James Mortimer.

"I observed it as you entered the room," said Holmes.

"It is an old manuscript."

"Early eighteenth century, unless it is a forgery."

"How can you say that, sir?" asked Dr. James Mortimer.

"You have presented an inch or two of it to my examination all the time that you have been talking. It would be a poor expert who could not give the date of a document within a decade or so. You may possibly have read my little monograph upon the subject. I put that at 1730."

"The exact date is 1742." Dr. Mortimer said.

3. The Problem

C. Holmes' Intuition Show (No. 28):

Holmes has a characteristic that when he encounters difficult cases, he likes to meditate alone. That day, after Dr. Mortimer introduced the case, Holmes fell into deep thinking again and hoped that Watson would not go home all day. Watson tacitly gave up his apartment and did not return until nearly nine o'clock in the evening.

When Holmes saw Watson coming back, he amused Watson:"There is a delightful freshness about you, Watson, which makes it a pleasure to exercise any small powers which I possess at your expense. A gentleman goes forth on a showery and miry day. He returns immaculate in the evening with the gloss still on his hat and his boots.He has been a fixture therefore all day.He is not a man with intimate friends. Where, then, could he have been? Is it not obvious(referring to Watson staying in the club)?"

D. Holmes praised Dr. Mortimer's intuition:

Dr. Mortimer said in describing the case: "Sir Charles had evidently stood there for five or ten minutes."

"How do you know that?" asked Holmes.

"Because the ash had twice dropped from his cigar." Dr. Mortimer replied.

Sherlock Holmes said happily:"Excellent! This is a colleague, Watson, after our own heart." Is it natural that he should stand for five or ten minutes, as Dr. Mortimer, with more practical sense than I should have given him credit for, deduced from the cigar ash?"

4. Sir Henry Baskerville

5. Three Broken Threads

E. Tracking and anti tracking:

Holmes said that they were "very keen to monitor him (Henry), but they were also very worried about being seen by him." This is tracking and anti tracking, and its essence is the contest between observation field and anti observation field, intuition field and anti intuition field.

The stalker was a bearded man—Charles Baronet Butler Barrymore was also a bearded man.The stalker intentionally disguises himself as a steward in order to create the illusion that the stalked person is the steward. This is the tracker's anti observation and anti intuition.

F. Five Wonders:

Within two days after the violent death of Charles baronet, a series of strange events (suspicious type) that could not be explained for a while happened unexpectedly, which made Holmes frown and silent. Suspicion impels Holmes to make various "speculations"(speculative type):

1. A letter cut out from a newspaper;
2. A black bearded stalker in a buggy;
3. Loss of newly purchased brown high boots;
4. The disappearance of old black leather shoes;
5. New brown high boots that have been lost and recovered.

These doubts and speculations opened the way for the final detection of the case.

6. The Baskerville Hall

7. The Stapletons of Merripit House

G. Watson's Doubts:

Appointed by Holmes, Watson escorted Henry back to Baskerville Manor. First of all, Watson had doubts about Barrymore(doubt type, the same bellow), the housekeeper of the manor. His suspicions are well founded: 1.He has sideburns;2.Crying at his wife late at night and telling lies;3.Holmes sent a telegram asking the post office to send it to Barrymore to prove whether his "trick" on the manor had not been implemented.

Watson also wondered:

Was he at the behest of others or was he plotting by someone else?

What good will it do him to kill the Baskerville family heirs?

Was he responsible for the warning letter that was cut and pasted, or might someone have done it because he was determined to oppose his plot?

The only result is that Henry "guessed the motive", that is, the manor owner scared away, and Barrymore and his wife could get a permanent and comfortable home.

H. Watson and Stapleton Fight:

In this dialogue with Watson, Stapleton tried to get Holmes' opinions on the case from Watson's words, tone and content. It reflects his intuition field.

Watson: "You think, then, that some dog pursued Sir Charles, and that he died of fright in consequence?"

Stapleton: "Have you any better explanation?"

Watson: "I have not come to any conclusion."

Stapleton: "Has Mr. Sherlock Holmes?"

Watson: "I am afraid that I cannot answer that question."

Stapleton: "May I ask if he is going to honour us with a visit himself?"

Watson: "He cannot leave town at present. He has other cases which engage his attention."

After many years of following Holmes, Watson has really made great progress, and also "smelled" out of Stapleton's intuition field. Therefore, a counter intuitive field came to the fore, making Stapleton's expectations empty.

"What a pity! He might throw some light on that which is so dark to us.But as to your own researches, if there is any possible way in which I can be of service to you I trust that you will command me. If I had any indication of the nature of your suspicions or how you propose to investigate the case, I might perhaps even now give you some aid or advice." Stapleton had no choice but to round off its "field".

8. Dr. Watson's First Report

9. Dr. Watson's Second Report

I. Watson's Epiphany:

In this investigation, Watson had two epiphanies, and the former did not give correct enlightenment:

"The night was very dark, so that I can hardly imagine how he could have hoped to see anyone. It had struck me that it was possible that some love intrigue was on foot. That would have accounted for his stealthy movements and also for the uneasiness of his wife." This is the result of Watson's epiphany, which is seriously inconsistent with the facts.

...

A sudden idea occurred to me, and I took the candle from the trembling hand of the butler.

"He must have been holding it as a signal," said I. "Let us see if there is any answer." I held it as he had done, and stared out into the darkness of the night...."There it is!" I cried.It turned out to be the contact signal between him and the escaped prisoner's brother-in-law.

10. Extract from the Diary of Dr.Watson

11. The Man on the Tor

12. Death on the Moor

13. Fixing the Nets

J. Holmes Appreciates Portrait:

Holmes and Watson followed Henry to the hall where his ancestor's portrait was hung. Facing the portrait of Holmes, they said:"I know what is good when I see it, and I see it now. That's a Kneller, I'll swear, that lady in the blue silk over yonder, and the stout gentleman with the wig ought to be a Reynolds. They are all family portraits, I presume?"

We don't need to care that we can't write a good work or draw a good picture; We also don't care if we can't play a beautiful melody or sing a moving song. But as long as we have intuitive thinking, it can enable us to circle around poetry and pictures, comment on them, and say whether they are good or not; it can point out the performance and singing, make comments, and taste it good or bad. It is very easy for Holmes, the intuitive master, to comment on these portraits.

14. The Hount of the Baskervilles

15. A Retrospection

K. Holmes' Intuitive Investigation:

Sir Henry Baskerville received an anonymous message cut and pasted in a newspaper, and Holmes could tell that it was cut from the Times and the main comment. He observed that even if newspapers and newspapers have the same font, the quality of the type used is also very different. He said:"If any possible doubt remained it is settled by the fact that 'keep away' and 'from the' are cut out in one piece."

He also believed that "The detection of types is one of the most elementary branches of knowledge to the special expert in crime".What is more admirable is that he can also see that the tool used for newspaper clipping is not scissors, but nail clippers! He said that the blade of the scissors was so short that he had to cut the word "far away" twice.

Holmes was also curious about two signs, which are worth studying. First, in order to eliminate clues, the handwritten address was scrawled, for fear that his handwriting would be recognized by Henry; The use of the Times' cut and paste content reveals that this person is a well educated person, and the newspaper is rarely read by ordinary people. Second, the characters are different, indicating that the people who cut and paste are careless, excited or nervous, and tend to the latter. This leads to two questions: Why did he panic? Afraid of being bumped into—who?

Dr. Mortimer said that we had to "guess".

Holmes said that you would think it was a "guess", "but I am almost certain that this address has been written in a hotel."

"How in the world can you say that?" asked Dr. Mortimer

Holmes reasoned that, first of all, when writing a word, the pen tip caught the paper twice and spilled ink. It means that the pen tip is very rough. Secondly, the ink dried three times after writing such a short address, indicating that there was little ink in the bottle.

If you think about it, private pens and ink bottles are rarely like this, and it is even more unusual for these two situations to occur at the same time.

111

Through the above conjecture and reasoning, the current investigation direction is clear. Go to the hotels near Charing Cross Street to check the paper basket. As soon as you find the cut copy of The Times, you can find the person who sent this strange letter.

It is described in the work that Holmes took the letter and "carefully examining the foolscap, upon which the words were pasted, holding it only an inch or two from his eyes." Then he said, "I think we have drawn as much as we can from this curious letter..."

In fact, the author buried the foreshadowing, leaving the suspense behind. After close observation, Holmes made a new discovery and smelled the perfume of white jasmine. In his case handling experience, more than one case was solved by identifying the type of perfume. "The scent suggested the presence of a lady, and already my thoughts began to turn towards the Stapletons. Thus I had made certain of the hound, and had guessed at the criminal before ever we went to the west country."

Holmes asked Henry Baskerville if "anything unusual" had happened. Henry remembered a trivial matter: a newly bought brown high-heeled boot had been stolen before he wore it.

"It seems that the stolen item is useless if it is not paired." Holmes asked the story of the high boots in detail and said: "I admit that I have the same idea (guess) as Dr. Mortimer. The lost leather shoes may be found soon."

Dr. Mortimer thought that the boots might not know where to put them, but they might be found after returning to the hotel.

Out of the detective's professional mindset, Holmes thought that the high boots might be used as a source of smell. When a new shoe was found, it would lose its function and would be returned or even replaced.

"Strange things" happened again. One of the old black boots was lost, and then the new one was "found" under the cupboard.

These "strange events" all confirmed Holmes' investigation process from reasonable doubt to correct speculation.

L. The Sense of Field Between Watson and Holmes:

Holmes, especially Watson, felt the existence of an invisible field everywhere in the process of detecting this case....

1. Holmes: "That means that while they are, as we have seen, very anxious to watch him, they are equally anxious that he should not see them. Now, this is a most suggestive fact."

2. Watson: "It was all dim and vague, but always there is the dark shadow of crime behind it."

3. Watson: "Consider the long sequence of incidents which have all pointed to some sinister influence which is at work around us."

4. Watson:"There's foul play somewhere, and there's black villainy brewing, to that I'll swear! Very glad I should be, sir, to see Sir Henry on his way back to London again!"

5. Watson: "Always there was this feeling of an unseen force, a fine net drawn round us with infinite skill and delicacy, holding us so lightly that it was only at some supreme moment that one realized that one was indeed entangled in its meshes."

6. Holmes: "My nets are closing upon him, even as his are upon Sir Henry, and with your help he is already almost at my mercy."

7. Watson: "Already I seemed to see our nets drawing closer around that lean-jawed pike."

THE VALLEY OF FEAR

1. The Tragedy of Bernstein

A. Holmes and Watson Cracked the Code:

HOLMES RECEIVED A STRANGE PASSWORD LETTER FROM POLLOCK, WITH FIGURES AND WORDS mixed in. So, he and Watson tried to crack the password with reasoning and speculation. Holmes speculated: "It is clearly a reference to the words in a page of some book." "That is our point of departure."

Holmes said that at the beginning, the password letter is a capital "534". We can assume (commonly used in reasoning) that it is the page number of the password source. This is a very thick book. What does the second symbol "C2" mean?

Watson:"Chapter the second, no doubt."

Holmes: "Hardly that, Watson. You will, I am sure, agree with me that if the page be given, the number of the chapter is immaterial. Also that if page 534 finds us only in the second chapter, the length of the first one must have been really intolerable."

"Column!" Watson cried.

Holmes agreed. Then he asked: "So now, you see, we begin to visualize a large book, printed in double columns, which are each of a considerable length, since one of the words is numbered in the document as the two hundred and ninety-third. Have we reached the limits of what reason can supply?""

Watson estimated:"I fear that we have."

Holmes said no. Then he said:"So we have contracted our field of search to a large book, printed in double columns and in common use."

"The Bible!" Watson cried triumphantly.

Holmes denied it through reasoning, which is a book that Mauriati's followers seldom have at hand. In addition, there are so many versions of the Bible that it is difficult to imagine that both versions have the same page number. This is obviously a unified version of the book. He is sure that the 534 pages in his book are exactly the same as those in mine.

"Bradshaw!" Watson speculated again.

Bradshaw's words are refined, but his vocabulary is limited, so it is difficult to convey ordinary messages. Exclude Bradshaw's works. The dictionary is not suitable either. So, what other books are there? Holmes denied and asked again.

"An almanac!" Watson continued to speculate.

"Excellent, Watson! I am very much mistaken if you have not touched the spot." Holmes affirmed Watson's conjecture. However, the following work of guessing and translating cannot be straightened out. Disappointment enveloped their entire room.

Suddenly, Holmes had an epiphany and cried excitedly. He ran to the bookcase and took out a book with a yellow cover. He said: We used the new almanac, and Pollock probably used the old one.".

As expected, the content of the decipherment was straightened out. The content of the decipherment is:Some deviltry is intended against one Douglas.

B. Intuitive Perspective Tone:

1.There was no trace then of the horror which I had myself felt at this curt declaration; but his face showed rather the quiet and interested composure of the chemist who sees the crystals falling into position from his oversaturated solution.

"Remarkable!" said he. "Remarkable!"

"You don't seem surprised."

"Interested, Mr. Mac, but hardly surprised. Why should I be surprised?I receive an anonymous communication from a quarter which I know to be important, warning me that danger threatens a certain person. Within an hour I learn that this danger has actually materialized and that the person is dead. I am interested; but, as you observe, I am not surprised."

1. "That questioning gaze transformed itself suddenly into abrupt speech.Have you found anything out yet?" she asked.
2. "Was it my imagination that there was an undertone of fear rather than of hope in the question?"
3. "I mind that you said it was a splay-foot, and here's the explanation. But what's the game, Mr. Holmes—what's the game?"
4. "'Ay, what's the game?' my friend repeated thoughtfully."

The Sign of Four

"The main thing with people of that sort," said Holmes to Watson, "is never to let them think that their information can be of the slightest importance to you. If you do they will instantly shut up like an oyster. If you listen to them under protest, as it were, you are very likely to get what you want."

In "The Hound of the Baskervilless"

1. "You mean that the thing is supernatural?" asked Holmes.
   "I did not positively say so." Dr. Mortimer answered.
   "No, but you evidently think it." Holmes said.
2. I had seen enough of the contrary nature of the old sinner to understand that any strong sign of interest would be the surest way to stop his confidences.
   "Some poaching case, no doubt?" said I with an indifferent manner.
3. "When do you desire to go?" he asked coldly.
   "That is final," said Lestrade.
   "Yes, that is final," I involuntarily echoed.
   "It is final," said Holmes.Something in his tone caught my ear, and I turned to look at him.

In "The Blanched Soldier"
The old butler said: "He was always courageous. There's not a tree in the park, sir, that he has not climbed.Nothing would stop him. He was a fine boy—and oh, sir, he was a fine man."

Dodd sprang to his feet. "Look here!You say he was. You speak as if he were dead. What is all this mystery? What has become of Godfrey Emsworth?"

In ancient China, there was a story about Yu Boya breaking the zither to thank his bosom friend. Although this is just a beautiful legend, it tells us that sound can transmit thoughts, feelings and emotions. However, how can we correctly interpret the rich connotation of sound? It depends on our intuitive ability, because it has the function of penetrating clouds and fog and understanding things.

Our ancestors also studied people's voices very much. *Yizhoushu Audio & Visual Chapter* points out that: people with a guilty heart falter in their voice, honest people speak with a clear rhythm, mean, perverse and insincere people speak with a harsh voice, and people with a broad and soft heart speak with a gentle voice, which is like that of a trickle.

Zeng Guofan not only studied people's appearance, but also their voice. He said, "The voice of a man is like the air of heaven and earth. If you are calm, your voice will be calm; if you are smooth, your voice will also be smooth."

Although it is difficult to find scientific basis for these classical statements of the ancients, they are the accumulation of life and work experience of predecessors and provide us with a valuable theoretical basis to distinguish voices.

When we analyze the voice, including the look, eyes, and appearance, we should not simply copy mechanically. We must integrate the specific situation and context at that time to obtain the true content. Otherwise, it is possible to miss a thousand miles, not only can not correctly analyze the original meaning, or even misunderstand, distort the original meaning, and go astray.

The common sounds are mainly tone, laughter and crying.

The tone is the tone, speed and intonation of people's speech. When people speak, their voices are either high or low, light or heavy, fast or slow, as well as the voice of desire to speak and stop, and the language potential always accompanied, all contain rich connotations, depending on whether we can correctly interpret them.

For example:"You mean that the thing is supernatural?" asked Holmes.

"I did not positively say so." Dr. Mortimer answered.

"No, but you evidently think it." Holmes said.

This is Sherlock Holmes' conclusion based on his interpretation of the meaning contained in his conversation with Dr. Mortimer.

In "The Blanched Soldie," Dodd clearly heard something bad from the tone of the old housekeeper: his friend Godfrey may be involved in some criminal case, or something dishonourable, involving the honor of the family. The strict father sent his son away or hid him to avoid the scandal.

Some studies believe that people's voice also contains the following contents: speed of speech depends on reaction, and voice size depends on confidence; Those who speak solemnly and deeply are knowledgeable, while those who speak sharply and severely are aggressive; Those who speak meekly are gentle and generous, while those who speak impetuously are grumpy and irritable. Whether it is accurate or not, we need to test it in our life and work, and we need to constantly analyze and enrich it with our own experience.

Laughter, a human instinct, is one of the oldest ways of communication between people.Laughter can also interpret people's thoughts and feelings. Some studies believe that laughter in different forms contains different personalities of people:cover your belly with your hands and laugh, broad-minded, with a sense of humor;smile quietly, introverted, shy and thoughtful;cover your mouth with your hands and smile, reserved, gentle and shy;silent smile, introverted sensibility, deep depression;smile secretly, conservative and depressed;smile scornfully, a cold disposition, and a keen observation;bright smile, sincere and warm, decisive and quick;laugh up and down, be outspoken and helpful;tears were laughed out, feeling rich and optimistic.

Laughter has many kinds, forms and connotations, which are too numerous to enumerate.For example, an elegant smile is a natural smile, a sincere smile is a smile from the heart, a happy smile is a sweet smile, a happy smile is a cheerful smile, a joyful laugh is talking and laughing at the same time, a shy smile is a smile with the head down, a moving smile is a tearful smile, humorous laughter is when others laugh at themselves, a loud laugh is a laugh that sets the whole room roaring, a confident smile is a loud laugh, an arrogant smile is a disdainful smile, a stupid smile is a silly smile, a stubborn smile is a bitter smile, a smile that pretends to be emotional is a fake smile, a complex laughter is laughing while crying, an embarrassed smile is a shy smile, a terrible smile is a foxy smile, an offensive laugh is a wild laugh, a ridicule is a laughter that brings unwell feeling, a malicious smile is a sneer, a disgusting smile is an obscene smile, a sinister smile is a cruel smile, a sad smile is a laugh after crying, a horrible smile is a sly smile.A correct interpretation of the connotation of human laughter is an accurate interpretation of human thought.

In this work, shortly after Douglas was killed, Watson was deeply worried and uneasy about his wife's laughter on some occasions, but he did not understand the other meanings behind the laughter:

1. Here within a few hours of the tragedy were his wife and his nearest friend laughing together behind a bush in the garden which had been his. I greeted the lady with reserve. I had grieved with her grief in the dining room. Now I met her appealing gaze with an unresponsive eye.
2. "She must be a heartless creature to sit laughing at some jest within a few hours of her husband's murder."

Holmes, on the other hand, saw something unusual through Mrs. Douglas's laughter instead of crying:It was badly stage-managed; for even the rawest investigators must be struck by the absence of the usual feminine ululation. If there had been nothing else, this incident alone would have suggested a prearranged conspiracy to my mind." Sure enough, Holmes took this as a clue to uncover a hidden farce directed by Douglas, participated by his wife and Buck.

In ancient China, there was a well-known story —Zi Chan listened to the voice, but he heard something unusual from the cry. One day, when Zichan was traveling, he heard a woman's cry and thought it was unreasonable (doubtful). He speculated that there might be hidden secrets. In order to find out the truth, they sent someone to bring her for interrogation, and at the same time, they carried out a forensic examination of the body. As Zichan suspected, she killed her husband only after having an affair.

Crying is also a human instinct and a form of expression of extreme emotions. It also contains rich connotations that need us to reveal.

The voice, laughter and cry contain both abnormal human psychology and other contents that need to be seen through. As the saying goes, "Listen to the voice when talking, and listen to the sound when playing drums and gongs". It is also one of the important tasks of intuition to listen to the "implied meaning".

C. Holmes Emphasized the Significance of Knowledge and Experience in the Investigative Work:

Holmes said earnestly to Sheriff MacDonald:"Mr. Mac, the most practical thing that you ever did in your life would be to shut yourself up for three months and read twelve hours a day at the annals of crime. Everything comes in circles–even Professor Moriarty."

Holmes also said: "Breadth of view, my dear Mr. Mac, is one of the essentials of our profession. The interplay of ideas and the oblique uses of knowledge are often of extraordinary interest."

Holmes put forward a request to the investigation work, to constantly expand the breadth and depth of the individual information database, and to turn himself into a "generalist" with a wide range of knowledge. Because "generalists" can make people think broadly and understand by analogy; It is easy for "professionals" to go all the way to the dark and get into a dead end.When Holmes evaluated the famous French detective Francois Le Villard in "The Sign of Four," he said that to be an excellent detective, he needs three conditions. He has two abilities, namely, insight and inference. Only "he lacks the extensive knowledge necessary for improving technology".However, extensive knowledge cannot be achieved overnight. It must be accumulated through time.

On the one hand, intuitive thinking is based on knowledge and experience. It requires the subject to have enough "extensive" knowledge and experience, which can better stimulate the subject's intuitive thinking; on the other hand, the investigation targets involve all walks of life, involving a very wide range of knowledge, and professional knowledge alone is far from enough. The richer the knowledge and experience, the more comfortable the intuitive thinking. Therefore, the rationality and richness of the human brain storage information database not only directly affect the speed of intuitive thinking, but also directly affect the accuracy of intuitive thinking.

In "A Study of Scarlet," we have seen the list of Sherlock Holmes' knowledge structure listed by Watson. It can be said that Holmes covers a wide range of subjects, with different depths and focuses on practicality.

Watson also introduced Holmes' practice of establishing archives, "For many years he had adopted a system of docketing all paragraphs concerning men and things, so that it was difficult to name a subject or a person on which he could not at once furnish information."

Holmes said:"I am an omnivorous reader with a strangely retentive memory for trifles."" I hold a vast store of out-of-the-way knowledge without scientific system, but very available for the needs of my work.Because of this, although the "lion mane" is ""as abstruse and unusual as any which I have faced in my long professional career", the answer is still found in an inconspicuous book. Only in this way can all kinds of knowledge accumulated in the investigation work be comprehended and used easily.

When Professor Li Meijin, who is known as the first person of Chinese psychological portrait, talked about how to improve the accuracy of "portrait", she said that it would require a lot of basic research and practical experience, depending on the degree of knowledge.Criminal psychology involves a wide range of knowledge. In terms of psychology alone, there are six disciplines that need to be studied as a basis: general psychology, social psychology, developmental psychology, physiological psychology, neuropsychology, and abnormal psychology.Then it involves the history of psychology and research methods of psychology.This is not about six or seven books, but about so many subjects, which are very different. For example, experimental psychology, which is completely physical, needs to make a situational hypothesis, and then verify the relationship between a behavior and a variable;physiological psychology is related to medicine, and it should study the nervous system.In addition, we should also study criminal psychology, as well as criminal law, jurisprudence, procedural law and evidence science. Otherwise, you don't know what to analyze when you analyze a case.Then there is the study of criminology, including a series of disciplines such as criminal sociology and criminal biology.Finally, it also involves criminal investigation, including scene, forensic medicine, trace, inspection...

Liu Feng, a criminal psychology expert of Wuhan Public Security Bureau, who is known as "a versatile person".miscellaneous family", has become famous in the field of psychological portrait in the investigation field. His first degree was in physics, but he studied philosophy, Chinese medicine, astronomy, radio, psychology, etc; he is interested in musical instruments, vocal music and opera; diligent in thinking, eloquent, and good at identifying and appointing people. It is precisely because of his extensive involvement that he has forged a three-dimensional and dialectical way of thinking. In addition, he has more than 20 years of practical experience in criminal investigation, so his accuracy of case inference is particularly high.

Holmes also said to Inspector MacDonald: "You will excuse these remarks from one who, though a mere connoisseur of crime, is still rather older and perhaps more experienced than yourself." Here Holmes raised the importance of experience to investigation.

Indeed, both logical investigation and intuitive investigation are inseparable from rich and sophisticated experience. This is especially true of intuitive thinking.

Intuition - investigative thinking is not only related to personal experience, occupation, education background, but also to personal temperament type.

People with professional backgrounds in politics, law, discipline inspection and supervision, and military are more accustomed to using intuitive thinking. In particular, due to the needs of work, political and legal personnel cannot communicate with ordinary criminal offenders who mainly use intuition to think without good intuitive thinking ability.

On the way to deal with the case in the countryside, Holmes said to Watson, "You look at these scattered houses, and you are impressed by their beauty. I look at them, and the only thought which comes to me is a feeling of their isolation and of the impunity with which crime may be committed there." This is the directional thinking of career cultivation.

Dr. Li Changyu said: I used to be a policeman. In my long career, I have established a reliable and effective system to insight into human nature and interpersonal relationships (the core of intuition). With the help of this system, I can accurately depict a person's personality without using tools such as lie detector or various psychological tests. The profession of police also sharpens people's intuition.

Duty criminals are a special criminal group. They used to be high-ranking public servants and even leading cadres. Their thinking level and perspective can be said to be totally different from that of ordinary criminal offenders. However, the level and perspective of thinking will gradually change after becoming a prisoner. Therefore, the thinking of duty criminals is multidimensional. The thinking form and way of duty criminals can also be found from their experience and educational background.

The thinking of people with high and low educational qualifications can be said to be a double heaven of ice and fire. If logical thinking is the core of IQ, then intuitive thinking is the soul of EQ. From the perspective of thinking, if the information is roughly divided into the symbolic information dominated by words (numbers) and the social information dominated by people and events, generally speaking, people with high IQ prefer to fly freely in the sky of symbolic information, but navigate hard in the sea of people and events. On the contrary, people with high EQ can swim with ease in the ocean of people and things, but stumble in the sky of symbols. Generally speaking, education background and intuitive thinking ability are often inversely proportional. The higher the education background is, the lower the intuitive thinking ability is, and the lower the education background is, the higher the intuitive thinking ability is.

In real life, we can often see this phenomenon. People with high education tend to treat people and things as lightly as possible when dealing with the relationship between people and things; However, those with low educational background (such as the leading cadres of the older generation of workers, peasants and soldiers, and those with high educational background on the job) can handle the above relationship with ease and delicacy.

Therefore, the true high IQ should include high EQ. Only when IQ and EQ keep pace with each other, intuition and logical thinking are both in perfect harmony, can people not only fight against the sky in symbolic information, but also ride the waves in the ocean of social information. This is the real "compound" talent.

The vast majority of ordinary criminal offenders are those with low educational background. They have long been in the society, experienced and familiar with the society, forming their inherent knowledge and experience structure, which is the basis of their thinking. If the police with high education are the counterpart, their thinking bases are far from each other, the results of their thinking will be very different, and the accuracy of their thinking will be greatly reduced. This disparity and asymmetry are particularly prominent in the trial of cases.

A large number of facts have also proved that many policemen who are active in the front line of the fight against criminals and have made achievements rarely have professional background or high education. This also raises a directional question for the relevant departments. Whether the local police academies are to train students who follow the rules and behave cautiously, or to cast brave and resourceful soldiers, the latter is undoubtedly more suitable for this group. The front-line police need not emphasize the high threshold of non undergraduate and non professional. Rich and extensive social experience is the indispensable wealth of investigators. In reality, the professional backgrounds of outstanding policemen who are active in the front line of investigation are varied. It is a good way to select excellent personnel from the auxiliary police to join the police force.

The perspective of thinking varies with different experiences. "A thousand people have a thousand Hamlets in their hearts". Intuitive thinking is based on experience, and experience will certainly guide the conclusion of intuitive thinking.

In addition, different temperament types also have a certain relationship with intuitive thinking. People with blood and bile are enthusiastic, lively and quick to talk, and the conclusion type is used more frequently; people with mucus and depression are calm, slow, and thoughtful, so suspicious or speculative types are more common among them.

Of course, in today's highly developed science and technology, high-tech crimes and high IQ crimes also test the depth of knowledge of investigators. Therefore, the cultivation of intuitive thinking must start with the expansion of the breadth of the individual information database, which is the needs of the subject and object of the investigation work. At the same time, when individuals have the ability, increasing the depth of individual information database will also help to detect crimes at a higher level.

D. Wife's Intuition:

Mrs. Douglas said:"Can a husband ever carry about a secret all his life and a woman who loves him have no suspicion of it?

She guessed out Douglas's secret from many details:

Avoid talking about some fragments of his life in America;

Some safety precautions taken by him;

Some of his occasional utterances;

From the way he looked at some uninvited guests.

Therefore, she was absolutely sure that the enemies he faced were powerful, and he knew that they were tracking him, and he was always on guard against them. Because of this, in recent years, as long as he came back later than expected, she was very frightened.

2. The Scowrers

HIS LAST BOW

1. Wisteria Lodge

A. Watson's intuition:

"A MEASURED STEP WAS HEARD UPON THE STAIRS, AND A MOMENT LATER A STOUT, TALL, GRAY-whiskered and solemnly respectable person was ushered into the room. His life history was written in his heavy features and pompous manner. From his spats to his gold-rimmed spectacles he was a Conservative, a churchman, a good citizen, orthodox and conventional to the last degree. But some amazing experience had disturbed his native composure and left its traces in his bristling hair, his flushed, angry cheeks, and his flurried, excited manner."

Watson can "see" a person's identity from his face, attitude, hair, complexion and demeanor, in general, from his temperament and aura, which shows that Watson's intuitive ability has improved a lot.

B. Holmes' Micro Expression:

Watson said: "I could tell by numerous subtle signs, which might have been lost upon anyone but myself, that Holmes was on a hot scent."

Indeed, in order to accurately interpret human expressions, especially transient microexpressions, we should not only have a good observation-intuition ability, but also have a necessary understanding of the object of observation-thinking. It can be said that the deeper we understand the object of observation-thinking, the higher the accuracy of observation-intuition.It is because Watson, the "best friend", has a comprehensive understanding of Holmes that he can "see" Holmes: "As impassive as ever to the casual observer, there were none the less a subdued eagerness and suggestion of tension in his brightened eyes and brisker manner which assured me that the game was afoot." If he is "an casual observer" or someone unfamiliar with Holmes, he will think Holmes "as impassive as ever".

C. Holmes interprets the eyes:

When Holmes went to visit a very strange suspect, "...I seemed to read in his dark, deep-set, brooding eyes that he was perfectly aware of my true business."

Holmes read the other side's intention of his visit from the other side's eyes.

D. Intuition Praised by Holmes:

Inspector Baynes proudly talked about his investigation:

"I was sure Henderson, as he calls himself, felt that he was suspected, and that he would lie low and make no move so long as he thought he was in any danger. I arrested the wrong man to make him believe that our eyes were off him. I knew he would be likely to clear off then and give us a chance of getting at Miss Burnet."

Holmes laid his hand upon the inspector's shoulder.

"You will rise high in your profession. You have instinct and intuition," said he.

Baynes flushed with pleasure.

Holmes praised Baines' keen intuition, which at least contains the following meanings:

First, he found and affirmed that Henderson's people had been suspected by the police;

Second, the mistake of catching the wrong person has become an anti intuition field, which makes Henderson relax his vigilance;

Third, it is to create opportunities for Henderson to leave the villa in order to find Miss Burnett.

2. The Carboard Box

The Same Description of "Micro Expression" and "Micro Action":

Here, Holmes guessed the description of Watson's psychology through "micro expression" and "micro action", which is similar to "The Resident Patient" in "The Memoirs of Sherlock Holmes".

3. The Red Circle

Holmes' Speculation:

The landlady has recently moved in with a strange tenant who is generous and lives in seclusion.He usually doesn't meet the landlady when delivering meals, but writes notes when he has something to do. The landlady found Sherlock Holmes to solve her doubts. After listening to the landlady's introduction, Holmes said to Watson, "The first thing that strikes one is the obvious possibility that the person now in the rooms may be entirely different from the one who engaged them."

"Why should you think so?" asked Watson.

Sherlock Holmes said: The tenant once went out immediately after renting the room. When he came back, no one proved that the person who came back was the one who went out. In addition, the person who rented the room spoke English very well, but the person who wrote the note wrote "match" instead of "matches". I can imagine that "the word was taken out of a dictionary, which would give the noun but not the plural".

Sherlock Holmes' correct speculation laid the right direction for the investigation of the case.

4. The Bruce-Partington Plans

A. Lestrade's Inaccurate Intuition:

West, one of the safe keepers, fell to death beside the railway and found seven of the ten stolen secret submarine drawings on his body. Lestred, Holmes Brothers and Watson discussed the case together.

"It seems to me perfectly clear," said Lestrade. "I have no doubt at all as to what occurred. He took the papers to sell them. He saw the agent.They could not agree as to price. He started home again, but the agent went with him. In the train the agent murdered him, took the more essential papers, and threw his body from the carriage. That would account for everything, would it not?" As for his absence of train ticket, Lestrade said: "The ticket would have shown which station was nearest the agent's house. Therefore he took it from the murdered man's pocket."

"Good, Lestrade, very good," said Holmes. "Your theory holds together. But if this is true, then the case is at an end. On the one hand, the traitor is dead. On the other, the plans of the Bruce-Partington submarine are presumably already on the Continent. What is there for us to do?"

Apparently, Holmes did not approve of Lestrede's speculation. The investigation of the case also proved Lestrade's mistake. This is a simple speculation from phenomenon to phenomenon, and it is an inaccurate intuition.

B. Intuition Led Holmes to Find Another Way:

"Our scent runs cold here, and there is a vast gap between either hypothesis and the laying of West's body, with seven papers in his pocket, on the roof of a Metropolitan train. My instinct now is to work from the other end."

We know that intuitive thinking has a characteristic of being "rebellious".If logical thinking is compared to a girl who follows the rules and keeps to herself; then, intuitive thinking is like a rebellious and unruly boy.

5. The Dying Detective

Holmes' Anti Intuition Field:

Planter Calverton Smith killed his nephew in order to inherit the estate. In order to obtain evidence of homicide, Holmes also designed an anti intuitive field - the bitter meat trap, so as to make the murderer be brought to justice.

He did not eat for three days and nights, starving himself out of shape. When the landlady found Watson, she said:"He's dying, Dr. Watson.For three days he has been sinking, and I doubt if he will last the day. He would not let me get a doctor. This morning when I saw his bones sticking out of his face and his great bright eyes looking at me I could stand no more of it."

When Watson arrived at Baker Street, he saw Holmes looking really sad.The room was gloomy in the dim light.The thin and shriveled face on the bed had red eyes, flushed cheeks and black skin on its lips due to fever. His hands kept twitching and his voice was dumb and eager.In the few hours I spent with him, I could see that his body was getting worse and worse: the heat spots were becoming more and more obvious, the eyes shot from the deep dark sockets were more piercing, and cold sweat was rising on his forehead (of course, Holmes' superb makeup was also responsible for this).Not only that, he also said a lot of "nonsense": "Indeed, I cannot think why the whole bed of the ocean is not one solid mass of oysters, so prolific the creatures seem. Ah, I am wandering! Strange how the brain controls the brain! What was I saying, Watson?" "No doubt there are natural enemies which limit the increase of the creatures. You and I, Watson, we have done our part. Shall the world, then, be overrun by oysters?"

Holmes made himself look like he was dying of tropical disease. Holmes not only fooled his landlady Harrison, but also fooled Watson, the doctor.

Was Holmes really perfect? no, it wasn't. In front of Watson, there were the following leaks:

First, when Watson came to Holmes' apartment, he did not let Watson, who was a doctor, get close to him;

Second, when Watson was going to invite a famous tropical disease expert, "with a tiger-spring, the dying man had intercepted me", and quickly locked the door;

Third, when Watson was about to leave, Holmes said, "Not now, Watson, not now. It's four o'clock. At six you can go."

Fourth, when Watson was doing nothing and was about to pick up an ivory box, Holmes suddenly cried out: ""Put it down! Down, this instant, Watson–this instant, I say!" The voice was loud enough to be heard in the street.

Sherlock Holmes had a series of unusual words and deeds. "Stupid" Watson not only did not detect any abnormality, but also made a "reasonable" interpretation from the perspective of friends and doctors: these things left a very unpleasant impression on me. He was rough and excited for no reason, and his words were still so rude, which was far from his usual kind attitude! This showed how feverish his mind was. The destruction of a wise mind was most deplorable.

Due to the true character of the landlady and the passionate performance of Dr. Watson, Holmes fooled the murderer Calverton Smith, and finally led the snake out of the hole to let him appear. In Holmes' apartment, because of the good effect of anti intuition field, Calverton Smith not only skillfully admitted the fact that he killed his nephew, but also obtained the murder weapon with catapult device—the ivory box with catapult device. So far, Holmes' painstaking anti intuition field has been completed. He said excitedly, "Exactly! Well, Watson, you have done all that a good friend could. You can now disappear from the scene."

6. The Disappearance of Lady Frances Carfax

A. Holmes' Intuition Show (No. 30):

"But why Turkish?" asked Mr. Sherlock Holmes, gazing fixedly at Watson's boots.

"English," Watson thought he was talking about his boots, and answered in surprise, "I got them at Latimer's, in Oxford Street."

Holmes knew Watson had misunderstood him, so he reminded him, "The bath!" and added that he had taken a Turkish bath.

Watson admitted:"Because for the last few days I have been feeling rheumatic and old. A Turkish bath is what we call an alterative in medicine–a fresh starting- point, a cleanser of the system.""But the boots and the bath?"

Holmes explained:"Equally childish. You are in the habit of doing up your boots in a certain way. I see them on this occasion fastened with an elaborate double bow, which is not your usual method of tying them. You have, therefore, had them off. Who has tied them? A bootmaker–or the boy at the bath. It is unlikely that it is the bootmaker, since your boots are nearly new.Well, what remains? The bath. Absurd, is it not? But, for all that, the Turkish bath has served a purpose."

B. Holmes' Intuition Show (No. 31):

"It belongs to the same elementary class of deduction which I should illustrate if I were to ask you who shared your cab in your drive this morning."

Without waiting for Watson to speak, Holmes gave the reason why he didn't come back by car alone:

"You observe that you have some splashes on the left sleeve and shoulder of your coat.Had you sat in the centre of a hansom you would probably have had no splashes, and if you had they would certainly have been symmetrical.Therefore it is clear that you sat at the side."

Watson said yes.

C. Holmes' intuition:

Ms. Francis Calfax disappeared for many days. Holmes and Watson searched for many places without success. When they were at a loss, Holmes said: "All my instincts tell me that she is in London, but as we have at present no possible means of telling where..."

Ms. Frances Calfax is indeed in London and has been controlled by Slesinger.

THE CASE-BOOK OF SHERLOCK HOLMES

1. The Illustrious Client

Holmes' Concealment:

SHERLOCK HOLMES WAS ENTRUSTED BY A MYSTERIOUS CUSTOMER TO STOP THE MARRIAGE between General Mayville's only daughter and handsome rogue tycoon Baron Gruna, and was attacked by Baron Gruna's henchmen. The local newspaper reported that: "There are no exact details to hand, but the event seems to have occurred about twelve o'clock in Regent Street, outside the Cafe Royal. The attack was made by two men armed with sticks, and Mr. Holmes was beaten about the head and body, receiving injuries which the doctors describe as most serious. He was carried to Charing Cross Hospital and afterwards insisted upon being taken to his rooms in Baker Street."

In response to such a dilemma, Holmes adjusted his plan, changed his strategy, resorted to his own devices, hid his wits, and entered the field of concealment.

There are similarities and differences between field concealment and counterintuitive field. The difference is that the former is mostly passive while the latter is active; it is true and false to be in the same place, which interferes with the other party's audio-visual and thinking and makes them make a wrong judgment.

When Watson came to visit the injured Holmes, he asked Watson to exaggerate his injury as much as possible after he went out. He has a concussion. He is unconscious now. He can live for a week at most! The more serious it is, the better, for Baron Gruna will certainly try to come to him and inquire about the news.

The effect Holmes expected came out. On the sixth day, everyone thought Holmes was dying; on the seventh day, the newspaper reported that he had erysipelas.

"That," said Holmes, "is the very impression which I intended to convey."

Baron Gruner never defended Holmes again. Holmes also carefully arranged. With the cooperation of Watson and Baron Gruna's former girlfriend Miss Winter, he personally sneaked into Baron Gruna's study and got Baron Gruna's love (lewd) diary, the most powerful weapon that could make the stubborn general's only daughter rein in and change her mind.

2. The Blanched Soldier

A. Holmes' Intuition Show (No. 32):

"From South Africa, sir, I perceive."

"Yes, sir," he answered, with some surprise.

"Imperial Yeomanry, I fancy."

"Exactly."

"Middlesex Corps, no doubt."

"That is so. Mr. Holmes, you are a wizard."

Holmes smiled at his bewildered expression and explained:

"When a gentleman of virile appearance enters my room with such tan upon his face as an English sun could never give, and with his handkerchief in his sleeve instead of in his pocket, it is not difficult to place him. You wear a short beard, which shows that you were not a regular. You have the cut of a riding-man. As to Middlesex, your card has already shown me that you are a stockbroker from Throgmorton Street.What other regiment would you join?"

"You see everything." Dodd exclaimed.

B. Holmes' Intuition Show (No. 33):

What has been happening at Tuxbury Old Park?

"Mr. Holmes—!"

"My dear sir, there is no mystery. Your letter came with that heading, and as you fixed this appointment in very pressing terms it was clear that something sudden and important had occurred."

"Yes, indeed...."

C. Holmes' Speculation:

Holmes had three suspicions about Godfrey being imprisoned by his father: one was that he escaped because of crime, the other was that he was mentally disturbed and would not live in an insane asylum, and the third was that there was a certain disease that needed isolation. Then the three guesses were "sifted and balanced against each other."—mainly reasoning.

First, the theory of crime is untenable. There are no local criminal reports that have not yet been solved. If it is a crime that has not been exposed yet, it should be taken away or sent abroad from the perspective of family interests, rather than hidden at home.

Second, the possibility of mental disorder is higher. Another person in the hut may be the caretaker. But this kind of compulsion cannot be very strict, otherwise Godfrey would not go to see his friend. If accompanied by a doctor and reported to the authorities, it is legal to leave a lunatic at home. Why do you keep it so secret? Therefore, mental disorder cannot be established.

Third, although it seems strange, it may fully conform to the actual situation. Leprosy is a common disease in South Africa, and whitening is a common symptom of this disease. Due to special circumstances, Godfrey may be infected. In this way, the situation of his relatives was very embarrassing, and they did not want to hand him over to the leprosy hospital. In order not to be interfered by the authorities, secrets must be kept strictly. It is not difficult to find a loyal doctor to take care of the patient if appropriate remuneration is given, and there is no reason not to let the patient come out at night.

In addition, Holmes also found that Ralph, who was delivering food to the hut, was wearing gloves soaked in disinfectant, which even ruled out the last doubt.

3. The Three Gables

"A smile" Reveals the Secret:

Mrs. Mary Maberley, who lives in The Three Gables of Harrow Forest, is very depressed these days. A generous customer wanted to buy her villa and everything in it at a high price, including furniture, personal items and even the relics of his son who died young. This strange condition made Mrs. Marbury suspicious, so she wrote to Holmes for his advice. So Holmes took Watson to The Three Gables.

When Mrs. Maberley was introducing the situation, Holmes suddenly raised his hand to stop talking, then strode to the side of the door, opened the door and grabbed a tall and thin woman like a chicken. She screamed and struggled. She is Susan, the maid.

"I have been listening to her for the last five minutes, but did not wish to interrupt your most interesting narrative." Holmes said. Then he asked, "Did you, Mrs. Maberley, mention to anyone that you were going to write to me and consult me?" Mrs. Maberley said no, but suddenly remembered that Susan had sent the letter, and found that she had spoken to a man at the fence.

"Suppose I tell you that it was Barney Stockdale to whom you spoke?" said Holmes.

"Well, if you know, what do you want to ask for?" Susan answered.

"I was not sure, but I know now. Well now, Susan, it will be worth ten pounds to you if you will tell me who is at the back of Barney."

"Someone that could lay down a thousand pounds for every ten you have in the world."

"So, a rich man?(Then Susan smiled.) No; you smiled–a rich woman."

Susan's casual smile made Holmes's keen intuition catch the profound connotation behind it, so he readjusted his thinking and pointed out the direction for correctly solving the mystery: not only did he find out Susan's identity as an undercover agent at Mrs. Maberley's house, but also found out the fact that their backstage boss was a woman, Isadora Klein.

It turned out that Klein had fallen in love with Mrs.Maberley's son Douglas. Because they were not in the household, Klein refused Douglas's proposal. Douglas wrote a novel based on their love story. Because Klein was afraid that their story would become a topic of conversation in London, he wanted to find and destroy the manuscripts from the relics that Douglas had brought back to The Three Gables. As a result, a series of soul stirring stories occurred.

4. The Sussex Vampire

Holmes' Intuitive Investigation:

This is a strange case in which Ferguson's current Peruvian wife abused his ex-wife's son and his own son, and it is even said that he drank his own son's blood.

When the case was about to be revealed, Holmes said: "I had, in fact, reached it(conclusion type)before we left Baker Street, and the rest has merely been observation and confirmation."

Let's look back at Sherlock Holmes' investigation process and how he confirmed his "conclusion" step by step.

Holmes inquired about the visiting Ferguson and learned that his wife's maid should know more about his wife's character than he did, Holmes made a special record;when Holmes learned that Ferguson's ex-wife's child was disabled but precocious, and had a deep relationship with Ferguson and his biological mother, Holmes recorded it again, and "lost his mind for a while." therefore, Holmes "made some assumptions ("assumptions" are speculations about the causes of things and their development and changes based on existing materials and experience, so we can also" speculate "and" guess "here), which will be refuted by time or new materials (It refers to the allegation that Ferguson's wife abused his ex-wife's son and his own son. In other words, it is to confirm his assumption that Ferguson's wife may not have abused two children).

Accompanied by Ferguson, Holmes and Watson went to the Ferguson's manor for field investigation. Entering the hall, I saw a row of South American vessels and weapons hanging on the top half of the wall, which should have been brought by Mrs. Ferguson Peru. Sherlock Holmes looked at these things carefully, and his eyes were full of contemplation— obviously it was Sherlock Holmes who was looking for the basis for his speculation.

Suddenly, a lame poodle came and aroused Holmes' curiosity(guessing type, the same below). It is understood that it was caused by an overnight illness four months ago. Even veterinarians can't figure out what the cause is.This strange event confirmed Holmes's "assumption".Then Holmes went again to study the various objects hanging on the wall.

They saw Ferguson and his ex-wife's son Jack. Watson described him like this:The youth looked at us with a very penetrating and, as it seemed to me, unfriendly gaze.That is to say, Jack's intuitive ability is very sharp, which probably shows the purpose of their trip. Some disabled people tend to have strong intuition. Holmes saw Ferguson fondling Jack when he was a baby. "I saw such jealousy, such cruel hatred, as I have seldom seen in a human face."

They also saw Ferguson's youngest son and the little red scar on his neck. Holmes was very attentive. His face was as still as a tooth carving. After looking at Ferguson and his son, he stared at something in the opposite direction curiously. "Following his gaze I could only guess that he was looking out through the window at the melancholy, dripping garden." But the window was half closed and nothing could be seen, but his eyes were clearly staring at the window—presumably he was thinking about the lame dog that had limped overnight. Then he smiled and his eyes returned to the baby. Holmes observed the baby's wound without saying a word. Then he said, ""Good-bye, little man. You have made a strange start in life."—Guess he found a connection between the lame dog and the baby.

At last, Holmes, Watson and Ferguson came to Ferguson's wife's bedroom together. Holmes exposed the case in front of everyone - his correct guess.

"A South American household. My instinct felt the presence of those weapons upon the wall before my eyes ever saw them."——This is to emphasize the undoubted tone. The real meaning is still to speculate: it may be other poisons, but he first thought of the poison arrows in South America. When Holmes saw the empty arrow box next to the bird's bow, he thought his guess was established.

If the baby is injured by the poisonous arrow dipped in nux vomica, it will be fatal if the poison is not sucked out immediately—this is the saying that the nurse Mrs. Mason and Ferguson saw the wife sucking the blood of her own son.

This reminded me of the lame dog. It was the test object before the man used the poison. Who was this person?

This man is actually Ferguson's eldest son, Jack. His whole soul was full of hatred for the baby, and the baby's fitness just reflected his disability and defects. This is an exaggerated and morbid love for his father and his dead mother, and these distorted love constitute his motivation.

5. The Three Garridebs

A. Holmes' Intuition Show (No. 33):

A business card was printed with "John Garrideb, Counsellor at Law, Moorville, Kansas, U. S. A." The client with an American accent came to Baker Street Apartment. Holmes had just determined the identity of the caller and said, "But surely you have been in England some time?""

"Why do you say that, Mr. Holmes?" The visitor said suspiciously.

"Your whole outfit is English." Holmes replied.

Mr. Garrideb forced a laugh. "I've read of your tricks, Mr. Holmes, but I never thought I would be the subject of them. Where do you read that?"

"The shoulder cut of your coat, the toes of your boots—could anyone doubt it?"

B. Holmes' Three Doubts:

After John, the client, introduced his entrustment, Holmes used three strange things to express his doubts about the matter. "I am wondering(dubious type, the same below), Watson—just wondering!"

"At what?" asked Watson.

"I was wondering, Watson, what on earth could be the object of this man in telling us such a rigmarole of lies." Then Holmes went back to his reasons for doubt:

First, after more than a year of wearing a frayed British coat and bent knees of British trousers, both in the letter and in his dictation, he said that he was an American who had just arrived in Britain;

Second, he said that he had not posted his notice in the missing person column. Holmes often browsed these columns out of professional needs;

Third, Holmes deliberately fabricated that a friend named Dr. Starr, the mayor of Topeka in the United States, was also believed.

The content, identity and words of John's commission are full of flaws. What exactly did he do, and what was the motive for pretending to look for Garridebs? This is worthy of our attention. Due to Holmes' reasonable and accurate suspicion, it points out the right direction for the investigation of the mystery.

6. The Problem Of Thor Bridge

Holmes' Doubts and Insight revealed the Case:

The wife of Gibson, a financial giant, was shot in the head by a pistol bullet on the garden nearly half a mile away from the house. At night, she wore evening dress and shawl. No weapons were found nearby, and there were no clues to murder at the scene.

Holmes said that from the existing evidence, he could only "suspect the governess", Dunbar.

First, the police found a one shot pistol in her wardrobe with the same caliber as the bullet in the body;

Second, the deceased had a note on her body, asking her to meet at the bridge, signed by the governess Dunbar;

Third, Dunbar went to Thor Bridge—the place where the case occurred shortly before the accident. The villagers who passed by also saw her there.

Watson said:"That really seems final."

""And yet, Watson–and yet!..." Holmes hesitated. Apparently, his intuition believed that the case was not that simple. His subsequent investigation showed the problem.

He thought that the pistol in Dunbar's wardrobe seemed to be bad for her, but it was actually the best.He said:After you committed the crime, instead of throwing the pistol into the reed pond to destroy it, you carefully took it home and put it in your closet, knowing that it was a place that had to be searched? Holmes said: "When once your point of view is changed, the very thing which was so damning becomes a clue to the truth. For example, there is this revolver. Miss Dunbar disclaims all knowledge of it. On our new theory she is speaking truth when she says so. Therefore, it was placed in her wardrobe. Who placed it there? Someone who wished to incriminate her. Was not that person the actual criminal?"

Secondly, the deceased had a note in his hand, asking her to meet at the bridge, signed by governess Dunbar. Why did the deceased still hold the note in his hand? She doesn't have to go to the cops during the meeting, does she? Isn't that strange? Obviously, they are eager to make it easy to find the note, and they still have the note in their dead hands. This alone should have aroused my suspicion earlier.

In addition, Holmes found traces of fierce attack on the stone railing at the scene, which made him puzzled. When he asked Dunbar to explain the situation, she thought it was "coincidence". Holmes did not agree and kept sighing: "But it was very strange, Miss Dunbar, very strange. Why did it happen at the time and place of the accident?" A series of questions puzzled Holmes.

Suddenly he sprang from his chair, vibrating with nervous energy and the pressing need for action.

"Never mind, my dear lady. You will hear from me, Mr. Cummings. With the help of the god of justice I will give you a case which will make England ring. You will get news by to-morrow, Miss Dunbar, and meanwhile take my assurance that the clouds are lifting and that I have every hope that the light of truth is breaking through." Obviously, this is the scene of Holmes' epiphany. He found a golden road in the fog.

This insight guided Holmes and his colleagues to the scene of the crime to do an investigation experiment. The experiment proved that this was a tragedy in which the wife of a financial giant was jealous, directed and acted by herself and blamed others.

7. The Creeping Man

A. Solve the Mystery Through Many Doubts:

Presbury, a famous Camford physiologist, was bitten by his own beloved wolf dog for many times. Mr. Bennett, the assistant of the professor and the son-in-law to be, turned to Holmes for help anxiously. Everyone thought it was weird. There are nine things related to the word "curious" or other word with similar meaning, including six from Holmes, one from the professor's daughter Edith, and two from Watson's narration.

Holmes:

"You never learn that the gravest issues may depend upon the smallest things. But is it not on the face of it strange that a staid, elderly philosopher—you've heard of Presbury, of course, the famous Camford physiologist?"

"Well, that has to be considered. But he attacks no one else, nor does he apparently molest his master, save on very special occasions. Curious, Watson —very curious. But young Mr. Bennett is before his time if that is his ring. I had hoped to have a longer chat with you before he came."

"Certainly we must agree that the professor has every claim upon his loyalty and devotion. But it may best be shown by taking the necessary steps to clear up this strange mystery."

"Singular! Most singular!" he murmured. "These details were new to me, Mr. Bennett. I think we have now fairly gone over the old ground, have we not? But you spoke of some fresh developments."

Professor's daughter Edith:

"It was last night, Mr. Holmes. He had been very strange all day. I am sure that there are times when he has no recollection of what he does. He lives as in a strange dream. Yesterday was such a day. It was not my father with whom I lived. His outward shell was there, but it was not really he."

Watson:

"A moment later we were actually in his sanctum, and the mysterious scientist, whose vagaries had brought us from London, was standing before us. There was certainly no sign of eccentricity either in his manner or appearance, for he was a portly, large-featured man, grave, tall, and frock-coated, with the dignity of bearing which a lecturer needs."

A series of doubtful words illustrate the mystery of the case, which not only drives Holmes' strong desire to reveal secrets, but also stimulates the readers' irresistible curiosity.

B. Holmes' Intuition:

"I have the greatest confidence in her intuition."

This is Holmes's comment on the professor's daughter Edith after a one-sided acquaintance. I think it is mainly based on the following two points:

One is that she "is a bright, handsome girl of a conventional English type".

The other is her filial piety to her father.

C. Holmes' Speculation:

"I expect the old gentleman has been putting two and two together," said Holmes as we walked to the hotel. "He struck me as having a particularly clear and logical brain from the little I saw of him. Explosive, no doubt, but then from his point of view he has something to explode about if detectives are put on his track and he suspects his own household of doing it. I rather fancy that friend Bennett is in for an uncomfortable time."

Holmes was right in his conjecture. Not only did he guess that the old professor had guessed their action and that his family had asked him to do so, but also he guessed that the assistant and son-in-law of the old professor had a hard time.

8. The Lion's Mane

A. Holmes' Intuition About Women:

Holmes said:"I value a woman's instinct in such matters." So, what are the main aspects of women's intuition "in such matters"? It is not mentioned in the work. It probably refers to people's emotions and interpersonal relationships rather than the case, because in this case, Maude's intuition proved wrong in the subsequent investigation.

Her boyfriend died inexplicably at the beach. Holmes came to investigate. She said:"Bring them to justice, Mr. Holmes. You have my sympathy and my help, whoever they may be." It seemed that she glanced defiantly at her father and brother as she spoke.

"Thank you," said Holmes. "I value a woman's instinct in such matters. You use the word 'they.' You think that more than one was concerned?"

Maud said:"I knew Mr. McPherson well enough to be aware that he was a brave and a strong man. No single person could ever have inflicted such an outrage upon him."

It is obvious that Holmes was misled by Miss Maude to believe that her boyfriend, Mr. McPherson, was harmed by "a group of people". The final investigation of the case proved that this "they" did not exist.

B. Holmes' Epiphany:

Holmes came to the place where Mr. McPherson died. His faithful Eldar hound also died here. When he came to the end of the path, he suddenly realized what he had been thinking about for a long time—a book called "Outdoors". The author was a famous nature observer. He found a highly toxic animal. The extended filamentous body could poison people and animals to death. Mr. MacPherson and his pet dog were killed by this animal.

C. Inspector Bader's intuition:

Inspector Bader basically believed that Murdoch was the murderer of his colleague MacPherson with a straight conscience.

First, Murdoch's character and his mystery are mainly manifested in his hot temper on the MacPherson puppy incident;

Second, he had quarreled with MacPherson in the past;

Third, he may resent MacPherson's pursuit of Miss Maude and take away his love.

However, these are basically superficial phenomena, and many situations have not been taken into account. Holmes questioned this:

1. He has alibi evidence. He was with the students, and he met us a few minutes after MacPherson appeared;
2. Don't forget, he can't deal with MacPherson alone;
3. What was the instrument used in the murder;
4. The dead man's last words were "lion's mane."

Inspector Bader had to admire:"You certainly do things thoroughly, Mr. Holmes."

9. The Veiled Lodger

Holmes Commented on Watson's Speculation:

Ron and his wife of the circus were attacked by their own domesticated lions. Ron died and his wife was injured. It is doubtful how the lion came out.

So Watson speculated about it—

The two of them went to feed the lion together. The lion suddenly came out, and they were ten meters away from the cage. The wife wanted to rush into the cage to close the cage door and protect herself. As soon as she got to the door, the lion knocked her down. She hated that her husband turned and ran away, which made the lion even more furious. If they fought against the lion, they might frighten it away. So she cried out, "Coward".

Holmes proposed that how did the lion come out when they were both ten meters away?

Watson said that maybe his enemy deliberately provoked the lion.

Holmes said:"Well, Watson, there is this to be said for your theory. Ronder was a man of many enemies. Edmunds told me that in his cups he was horrible.A huge bully of a man, he cursed and slashed at everyone who came in his way. I expect those cries about a monster, of which our visitor has spoken, were nocturnal reminiscences of the dear departed. However, our speculations are futile until we have all the facts.

10. S Hoscombe Old Place

Holmes' Inaccurate Speculation:

Sir Robert, the owner of Mr. Mason, the horse racing instructor, is an unmarried man. He lives in Shawscom Villa with his widowed sister, Mrs. Beatrice Fuld, and depends on his sister to help him. The sister and brother have a good relationship.

Mr. Mason, the instructor, told Holmes about a series of perplexities of his master:

First, Sir Robert almost madly bet all the money he could give out and borrow on the race horse Prince Shoscom. If Prince fails, he will go bankrupt.

Second, his sister Beatrice had the same interest in horses, and she would take a carriage to see the Prince on time every day. Recently, however, she seems to have lost interest in horses. She passed the horse pen for a week without looking at it.

Third, the two brothers and sisters have quarreled recently and become enemies. Robert also gave her sister's dog to the owner of the Green Dragon.

Fourth, why does Sir Robert often go to the crypt of the old church late at night? Who is the man waiting for him there?

Fifthly, an ankle bone was found in the heating boiler in the basement of Mrs. Beatrice's room.

On this basis, Holmes speculated:This case is not simple, Mr. Mason. It's bloody. therefore. Holmes brought Watson to the scene—Shoscom made a field investigation. According to the investigation, Holmes made another "scandalous supposition". Sir Robert may have killed his sister. To this end, they also made a small "experiment". When Mrs Beatrice leaves the carriage, let her pet dog out to test whether it is Mrs Beatrice or not. It turned out to be a fake Mrs Beatrice. Holmes' conjecture was "confirmed".

So what is the truth?

After meeting Sir Robert at the old church late at night, Holmes finally revealed a series of mysteries.

Sir Robert depended on his sister for everything, and her estate income was only enough for her own expenses. He knew that as soon as his sister died, his creditors would flock to his property like vultures, taking away his stables, horses and everything. Robert tamed a black horse "Prince" in order to participate in the horse race. If he wins, everything goes well. If you lose, the consequences will be unimaginable.In fact, his sister died of edema a week ago, and dare not tell anyone! If he could cover it up for three weeks, everything would be all right.His maid's husband is an actor. So he thought of making him act like his sister. Just show up in a carriage every day. Mrs Beatrice's doctor foreshadowed this outcome months ago. The first night after her death, Robert and Nolett transported her to the old warehouse. But her little dog kept following them, barking at the door. So Robert gave the puppy away and moved the body to the crypt of the church.

Holmes' intuition level is extraordinary. But it does not mean that all his thoughts can be impartial and hit one hundred shots at a time. This is the Sherlock Holmes who is popular in people's life.

11. The Retired Colourman

Holmes' Intuition on "Second-hand" Information:

We clearly remember that Holmes introduced his career to Watson in "A Study in Scarlet," saying that he was the only consulting detective in the world. Many official and unofficial detectives in London would come to him when they met difficulties. As long as they provided all clues and evidence, they could get satisfactory answers.

"But do you mean to say," Watson said, "that without leaving your room you can unravel some knot which other men can make nothing of, although they have seen every detail for themselves?"

Holmes said:"Quite so. I have a kind of intuition that way. Now and again a case turns up which is a little more complex."

This work is a successful case that depends on listening to the report, finding the investigation clues accurately and finally solving the case.

The client, a 61 year old retired pigment dealer, Josiah Ambley, married a beautiful woman 20 years younger than himself. They live well, have money and leisure, and should be a happy family. Within two years, however, Amberley had become an old man who was listless and lethargic. According to him, the reason is a very old story: a treacherous friend and a womanly woman.

Amber liked playing chess. Not far from him lived a young doctor, Ray Ernest, who was also a chess lover. He often went to Amber's house to play chess. He naturally became close to Mrs. Amber when he came and went, and they eloped last week. What's worse is that the cheating wife robbed all the valuable securities of Amberley. Now it is urgent to find the runaway wife and recover his property. As Holmes' case was at a critical moment, Watson was asked to go to Lewisham to learn about the case.

It was late that night when Watson returned to Baker Street for investigation. Holmes got stuck in the sofa and listened to Watson's report. Holmes heard that on the evening of Amberley's wife's elopement, he also booked tickets for the second row on the second floor of the Haymarket Theatre. After questioning, he learned that the seat number was 31. Holmes said:"Excellent, Watson! His seat, then, was either thirty or thirty-two." To this, Watson looked puzzled.When hearing that Amberley was painting the house, Holmes said alertly:"Does it not strike you as a strange occupation in the circumstances?" Of course, there were other situations.Holmes felt that these two clues were the key to the case, and decided to investigate in person from then on.

The results of the investigation proved that Holmes' intuition was right.After investigating the ticket sales form of the box office of the Haymarket Theatre, it was found that seats 30 and 32 in the second row of the box were empty that night, and Holmes could feel the seriousness of the case.Amberley lied, and what does it mean that he deliberately made alibi evidence?Amber was painting at home at this moment to cover up a certain smell with a strong smell of paint. What was the smell? It was probably "some guilty smell which would suggest suspicions".After on-site investigation, it was found that there was gas smell or even rotten smell.So far, there was no secret about all the situations.After Holmes' careful inspection of the house, he finally found out the fact that Amberley poisoned his wife and Dr. Ray Ernest through the gas pipe in a small room out of strong jealousy.

EXCERPT FROM HOLMES PERSONALITY DESCRIPTION

A. Sherlock Holmes in Watson's Eyes

OH, I DIDN'T SAY THERE WAS ANYTHING AGAINST HIM. HE IS A LITTLE QUEER IN HIS IDEAS—AN enthusiast in some branches of science. As far as I know he is a decent fellow enough.... He is well up in anatomy, and he is a first-class chemist; but as far as I know, he has never taken out any systematic medical classes. His studies are very desultory and eccentric, but he has amassed a lot of out-of-the-way knowledge which would astonish his professors. (From "A Study in Scarlet," Volume I, page 5)

Holmes was certainly not a difficult man to live with. He was quiet in his ways, and his habits were regular. It was rare for him to be up after ten at night, and he had invariably breakfasted and gone out before I rose in the morning. Sometimes he spent his day at the chemical laboratory, sometimes in the dissecting-rooms, and occasionally in long walks, which appeared to take him into the lowest ports of the city. Nothing could exceed his energy when the working fit was upon him; but now and again a reaction would seize him, and for days on end he would lie upon the sofa in the sitting-room, hardly uttering a word or moving a music from morning to night. On these occasions I have noticed such a dreamy, vacant expression in his eyes, that I might have suspected him of being addicted to the use of some narcotic, had not the temperance and cleanliness of his whole life forbidden such a notion. (From "A Study in Scarlet," Volume I, page 11)

His very person and appearance were such as to strike the attention of the most casual observer. In height he was rather over six feet and so excessively lean that he seemed to be considerably taller. His eyes were sharp and piercing, save during those intervals of torpor to which I have alluded; and his thin, hawk-like nose gave his whole expression an air of alertness and decision. His chin, too, had the prominence and squareness which mark the man of determination. His hands were invariably blotted with ink and stained

145

with chemicals, yet he was possessed of extraordinary delicacy of touch, as I frequently had occasion to observe when I watched him manipulating his fragile philosophical instruments.(From "A Study in Scarlet," Volume I, page 11)

He was not studying medicine. He had himself, in reply to a question, confirmed Stamford's opinion upon that point. Neither did he appear to have pursued any course of reading which might fit him for a degree in science or any other recognized portal which would give him an entrance into the learned world. Yet his zeal for certain studies was remarkable, and within eccentric limits his knowledge was so extraordinarily ample and minute that his observations have fairly astounded me. Surely no man would work so hard or attain such precise information unless he had some definite end in view. Desultory readers are seldom remarkable for the exactness of their learning. No man burdens his mind with small matters unless he has some very good reason for doing so.

His ignorance was as remarkable as his knowledge. Of contemporary literature, philosophy and politics he appeared to know next to nothing.(From "A Study in Scarlet," Volume I, page 12)

"This fellow may be very clever," I said to myself, "but he is certainly very conceited."(From "A Study in Scarlet," Volume I, page 19)

My marriage had drifted us away from each other. My own complete happiness, and the home-centred interests which rise up around the man who first finds himself master of his own establishment, were sufficient to absorb all my attention, while Holmes, who loathed every form of society with his whole Bohemian soul, remained in our lodgings in Baker Street, buried among his old books, and alternating from week to week between cocaine and ambition, the drowsiness of the drug, and the fierce energy of his own keen nature.He was still, as ever, deeply attracted by the study of crime, and occupied his immense faculties and extraordinary powers of observation in following out those clues, and clearing up those mysteries which had been abandoned as hopeless by the official police.(From "A Scandal In Bohemia," Volume I, page 239)

It was a singular document. Philosophy, astronomy, and politics were marked at zero, I remember. Botany variable, geology profound as regards the mud-stains from any region within fifty miles of town, chemistry eccentric, anatomy unsystematic, sensational literature and crime records unique, violin-player, boxer, swordsman, lawyer, and self-poisoner by cocaine and tobacco. Those, I think, were the main points of my analysis. (From "The Five Orange Hips," Volume I, pages 343 to 344)

I was repelled by the egotism which I had more than once observed to be a strong factor in my friend's singular character.(From "The Copper Beaches," Volume I, pages 492 to 493)

Sherlock Holmes was a man who seldom took exercise for exercise's sake. Few men were capable of greater muscular effort, and he was undoubtedly one of the finest boxers of his weight that I have ever seen;but he looked upon aimless bodily exertion as a waste of energy, and he seldom bestirred himself save where there was some professional object to be served. Then he was absolutely untiring and indefatigable. That he should have kept himself in training under such circumstances is remarkable, but his diet was usually of the sparest, and his habits were simple to the verge of austerity. Save for the occasional use of cocaine, he had no vices, and he only turned to the drug as a protest against the monotony of existence when cases were scanty and the papers uninteresting.(From "The Yellow Face," Volume I, page 547)

An anomaly which often struck me in the character of my friend Sherlock Holmes was that, although in his methods of thought he was the neatest and most methodical of mankind, and although also he affected a certain quiet primness of dress, he was none the less in his personal habits one of the most untidy men that ever drove a fellow-lodger to distraction. Not that I am in the least conventional in that respect myself. The rough-and-tumble work in Afghanistan, coming on the top of natural Bohemianism of disposition, has made me rather more lax than befits a medical man. But with me there is a limit, and when I find a man who keeps his cigars in the coal-scuttle, his tobacco in the toe end of a Persian slipper, and his unanswered correspondence transfixed by a jack-knife into the very centre of his wooden mantelpiece, then I begin to give myself virtuous airs. I have always held, too, that pistol practice should be distinctly an open-air pastime; and when Holmes, in one of his queer humours, would sit in an armchair with his hair-trigger and a hundred Boxer cartridges and proceed to adorn the opposite wall with a patriotic V. R. done in bullet-pocks, I felt strongly that neither the atmosphere nor the appearance of our room was improved by it.

Our chambers were always full of chemicals and of criminal relics which had a way of wandering into unlikely positions, and of turning up in the butter-dish or in even less desirable places. But his papers were my great crux. He had a horror of destroying documents, especially those which were connected with his past cases, and yet it was only once in every year or two that he would muster energy to docket and arrange them; for, as I have mentioned somewhere in these incoherent memoirs, the outbursts of passionate energy when he performed the remarkable feats with which his name is associated were followed by reactions of lethargy during which he would lie about with his violin and his books, hardly moving save from the sofa to the table. Thus month after month his papers accumulated until every corner of the room was stacked with bundles of manuscript which were on no account to be burned, and which could not be put away save by their owner.(From "The Musgrave Ritual," Volume I, pages 604 to 605)

During my long and intimate acquaintance with Mr. Sherlock Holmes I had never heard him refer to his relations, and hardly ever to his own early life. This reticence upon his part had increased the somewhat inhuman effect which he produced upon me, until sometimes I found myself regarding him as an isolated phenomenon, a brain without a heart, as deficient in human sympathy as he was preeminent in intelligence. His aversion to women and his disinclination to form new friendships were both typical of his unemotional character, but not more so than his complete suppression of every reference to his own people. I had come to believe that he was an orphan with no relatives living; but one day, to my very great surprise, he began to talk to me about his brother. (From "The Greek Interpreter," Volume I, page 682)

There were points about this strange business which would, I was sure, have specially appealed to him, and the efforts of the police would have been supplemented, or more probably anticipated, by the trained observation and the alert mind of the first criminal agent in Europe.(From "The Empty House," Volume I, pages 759 to 760)

I have never known my friend to be in better form, both mental and physical, than in the year '95. His increasing fame had brought with it an immense practice, and I should be guilty of an indiscretion if I were even to hint at the identity of some of [559] the illustrious clients who crossed our humble threshold in Baker Street. Holmes, however, like all great artists, lived for his art's sake, and, save in the case of the Duke of Holdernesse, I have seldom known him claim any large reward for his inestimable services. So unworldly was he—or so capricious—that he frequently refused his help to the powerful and wealthy where the problem made no appeal to his sympathies, while he would devote weeks of most intense application to the affairs of some humble client whose case presented those strange and dramatic qualities which appealed to his imagination and challenged his ingenuity.(From "The Adventure of Black Peter," Volume I, page 885)

Holmes had remarkable powers, carefully cultivated, of seeing in the dark.(From "The Adventure of Charles Augustus Milverton," Volume I, page 916)

Things had indeed been very slow with us, and I had learned to dread such periods of inaction, for I knew by experience that my companion's brain was so abnormally active that it was dangerous to leave it without material upon which to work. For years I had gradually weaned him from that drug mania which had threatened once to check his remarkable career. Now I knew that under ordinary conditions he no longer craved for this artificial stimulus, but I was well aware that the fiend was not dead but sleeping, and I have known that the sleep was a light one and the waking near when in periods of idleness I have seen the drawn look upon Holmes's ascetic face, and the brooding of his deep-set and inscrutable eyes. Therefore I blessed this Mr. Overton, whoever he might be, since he had come with his enigmatic message to break that dangerous calm which brought more peril to my friend than all the storms of his tempestuous life." (From "The Adventure of the Missing Three-Quarter," Volume I, page 988)

Holmes was accessible upon the side of flattery, and also, to do him justice, upon the side of kindliness.(From "The Adventure of the Red Circle," Volume II, page 378)

It was one of my friend's most obvious weaknesses that he was impatient with less alert intelligences than his own.(From "The Adventure of the Bruce-Partiongton Plans," Volume II, page 408)

His eager face still wore that expression of intense and high-strung energy, which showed me that some novel and suggestive circumstance had opened up a stimulating line of thought. See the foxhound with hanging ears and drooping tail as it lolls about the kennels, and compare it with the same hound as, with gleaming eyes and straining muscles, it runs upon a breast-high scent—such was the change in Holmes since the morning. He was a different man from the limp and lounging figure in the mouse-coloured dressing-gown who had prowled so restlessly only a few hours before round the fog-girt room.(From "The Adventure of the Bruce-Partiongton Plans," Volume II, page 409)

Mrs. Hudson, the landlady of Sherlock Holmes, was a long-suffering woman. Not only was her first-floor flat invaded at all hours by throngs of singular and often undesirable characters but her remarkable lodger showed an eccentricity and irregularity in his life which must have sorely tried her patience. His incredible untidiness, his addiction to music at strange hours, his occasional revolver practice within doors, his weird and often malodorous scientific experiments, and the atmosphere of violence and danger which hung around him made him the very worst tenant in London.

The landlady stood in the deepest awe of him and never dared to interfere with him, however outrageous his proceedings might seem. She was fond of him, too, for he had a remarkable gentleness and courtesy in his dealings with women. He disliked and distrusted the sex, but he was always a chivalrous opponent.(From "The Adventure of the Dying Detective," Volume II, pages 428 to 429)

To his sombre and cynical spirit all popular applause was always abhorrent, and nothing amused him more at the end of a successful case than to hand over the actual exposure to some orthodox official, and to listen with a mocking smile to the general chorus of misplaced congratulation.(From "The Adventure of the Devil's Foot" Volume II, page 465)

There was a curious secretive streak in the man which led to many dramatic effects, but left even his closest friend guessing as to what his exact plans might be. He pushed to an extreme the axiom that the only safe plotter was he who plotted alone. I was nearer him than anyone else, and yet I was always conscious of the gap between.(From "The Adventure of the Illustrious Client," Volume II, page 529)

He was a man of habits, narrow and concentrated habits, and I had become one of them.As an institution I was like the violin, the shag tobacco, the old black pipe, the index books, and others perhaps less excusable.(From "The Adventure of the Creeping Man," Volume II, page 653)

B. Holmes Saw Himself:

Let me see—what are my other shortcomings? I get in the dumps at times, and don't open my mouth for days on end. You must not think I am sulky when I do that. Just let me alone, and I'll soon be right.(From "A Study in Scarlet," Volume I, page 9)

I have a turn both for observation and for deduction. (From "A Study in Scarlet," Volume I, page 17)

Observation with me is second nature.(From "A Study in Scarlet," Volume I, page 18)

I know well that I have it in me to make my name famous. No man lives or has ever lived who has brought the same amount of study and of natural talent to the detection of crime which I have done. (From "A Study in Scarlet," Volume I, page 19)

My mind rebels at stagnation. Give me problems, give me work, give me the most abstruse cryptogram, or the most intricate analysis, and I am in my own proper atmosphere. I can dispense then with artificial stimulants. But I abhor the dull routine of existence. I crave for mental exaltation. That is why I have chosen my own particular profession, or rather created it, for I am the only one in the world.(From "The Sign of Four," Volume I, page 124)

It is of the first importance not to allow your judgment to be biased by personal qualities. A client is to me a mere unit, a factor in a problem. The emotional qualities are antagonistic to clear reasoning.(From "The Sign of Four," Volume I, page 135)

But love is an emotional thing, and whatever is emotional is opposed to that true cold reason which I place above all things. I should never marry myself, lest I bias my judgment."(From "The Sign of Four," Volume I, page 235)

Yes, there are in me the makings of a very fine loafer, and also of a pretty spry sort of a fellow. I often think of those lines of old Goethe:Schade, dass die Natur nur einen Mensch aus dir schuf, Denn zum würdigen Mann war und zum Schelmen der Stoff. (From "The Sign of Four," Volume I, pages 235 to 236)

I was never a very sociable fellow, Watson, always rather fond of moping in my rooms and working out my own little methods of thought, so that I never mixed much with the men of my year. Bar fencing and boxing I had few athletic tastes, and then my line of study was quite distinct from that of the other Fellows...(From "The Gloria Scott," Volume I, page 585)

When I first came up to London I had rooms in Montague Street, just round the corner from the British Museum, and there I waited, filling in my too abundant leisure time by studying all those branches of science which might make me more efficient.(From "The Musgrave Ritual," Volume I, pages 606 to 607)

I cannot agree with those who rank modesty among the virtues. To the logician all things should be seen exactly as they are, and to underestimate one's self is as much a departure from truth as to exaggerate one's own powers.(From "The Greek Interpreter," Volume I, page 683)

I have an impish habit of practical joking. Also that I can never resist a dramatic situation.(From "The Adventure of Mazarin Stone," Volume II, page 575)

Women have seldom been an attraction to me, for my brain has always governed my heart, but I could not look upon her perfect clear-cut face, with all the soft freshness of the downlands in her delicate colouring, without realizing that no young man would cross her path unscathed.(From "The Adventure of the Lion's Mane," Volume II, page 681)

参考文献:

[1]彭聃龄.普通心理学[M].北京:师范大学出版社,2015:263.

[2][美]布鲁纳著.教育过程[M].邵瑞珍译,北京:文化教育出版社,1982:16.

[3]董奇.论直觉思维.北京师范大学学报,1987,(1).

[4]王福相.论侦察思维的多元性和互补性].湖北公安高等专科学校学报,199,(5):43.

[5][英]阿瑟·柯南·道尔,陈羽纶、丁钟华等译. 福尔摩斯探案全集[M].北京:群众出版社,2014.6

[6][英]阿瑟·柯南·道尔,陈羽纶、丁钟华等译. 福尔摩斯探案全集[M].北京:群众出版社,1981.3

[7][英]阿瑟·柯南·道尔,郑红峰译. 福尔摩斯探案全集[M].长春:吉林出版集团有限公司,2015.5

[8][英]阿瑟·柯南·道尔,陶雅慧译注. 福尔摩斯探案全集[M].北京:中国文史出版社,2014.8

[9][英]阿瑟·柯南·道尔,余 芳译. 福尔摩斯探案集[M].广州:花城出版社,1915

[10][英]阿瑟·柯南·道尔,瑞 烨编译. 福尔摩斯探案集[M].海口:南海出版公司,2013.11

[11]唐旭东编著.神探侦查思维直觉透视[M]南昌:江西高校出版社,2020.10

[12]唐旭东编著.直觉的魅力[M]美国:南方出版社,2021.11

POSTSCRIPT

Master of Intuition:Sherlock Holmes, has finally come out!

There are several difficulties for me to study *Sherlock Holmes*: first, there are many pages and characters. The Chinese edition of *Sherlock Holmes* (translated by Chen Yulun, Ding Zhonghua, etc.) published by the Mass Publishing House in June 2014 has more than 1.53 million words. It takes me a lot of time to simply read it through once. To study it, it is necessary to read it twice or three times. Some key chapters even need to be read four or five times. Therefore, I had to invest a lot of time, especially energy, which was sometimes beyond the ability for an elderly person like me; second, I was unable to read the original text, so I had to buy five sets of Chinese translations to compare the key words and sentences. Although the effect was limited, it was better than nothing; third, in the process of reading, I was not used to the names of people and places in the translation, which undoubtedly increased the difficulty of memory and affects the reading speed; fourth, most importantly, my level of knowledge is very limited. In the face of the above difficulties, although I try to overcome them with a meticulous attitude and the will of leeches gnawing at the bones, there must be problems such as neglecting one thing and the other, and there may even be many essence and highlights that have not been found. I sincerely hope readers, especially experts and scholars, will forgive me and put forward valuable opinions!

After the completion of this book, the Chinese version was published by Inner Mongolia People's Publishing House of the People's Republic of China. In order to let more fans and researchers around the world see this book and hear their feedback, praise, criticism and scolding of my views, I thought of publishing the English version in due time. In the whole process, I was fortunate to have Mr. Wu Minghua's full help. Mr. Wu Minghua is the former vice president and deputy editor in chief of Jiangxi Education Press, and the winner of the National Book Award. His praise for this book has greatly encouraged my determination and interest in publishing the English version. Here, I would like to express my deep gratitude to Mr. Wu Minghua.

Printed in the United States
by Baker & Taylor Publisher Services